Kitchen & Bath Project Management

Installation ◆ Contractors ◆ Cost Controls

Ellen Cheever, CMKBD, ASID
With Paul Pankow, CKBI, MA

Professional Resource Library

This book is intended for professional use by residential kitchen and bath designers. The procedures and advice herein have been shown to be appropriate for the applications described; however, no warranty (expressed or implied) is intended or given. Moreover, the user of this book is cautioned to be familiar with and to adhere to all manufacturers' planning, installation and use/care instructions. In addition, the user is urged to become familiar with and adhere to all applicable local, state and federal building codes, licensing and legislation requirements governing the user's ability to perform all tasks associated with design and installation standards, and to collaborate with licensed practitioners who offer professional services in the technical areas of mechanical, electrical and load bearing design as required for regulatory approval, as well as health and safety regulations.

Information about this book and other Association programs
and publications may be obtained from the
National Kitchen & Bath Association
687 Willow Grove Street, Hackettstown, New Jersey 07840
Phone (800) 843-6522
NKBA.org

ISBN 1-887127-58-5

Second Edition 2010

Drawings and Illustrations by Karen Dorion

Cover photos by Larry A. Falke Photography—Lake Forest, CA
Special thanks to Room Scapes—Laguna Niguel, CA

Consulting and design by Fry Communications, Irvine, CA

Peer Reviewers

Timothy Aden, CMKBD	Jim Krengel, CMKBD
Julia Beamish, Ph.D, CKE	Chris LaSpada, CPA
Leonard V. Casey	Elaine Lockard
Ellen Cheever, CMKBD, ASID	Phyllis Markussen, Ed.D, CKE, CBE
Hank Darlington	Chris J Murphy, CKD, CBD, CKBI
Dee David, CKD, CBD	David Newton, CMKBD
Peggy Deras, CKD, CID	Roberta Null, Ph.D
Kimball Derrick, CKD	Michael J Palkowitsch, CMKBD
Tim DiGuardi	Paul Pankow, CKBI
Kathleen Donohue, CMKBD	Jack Parks
Gretchen L. Edwards, CMKBD	Kathleen R. Parrott, Ph.D, CKE
JoAnn Emmel, Ph.D	Al Pattison, CMKBD
Jerry Germer	Les Petrie, CMKBD
Pietro A. Giorgi, Sr., CMKBD	Becky Sue Rajala, CKD
Tom Giorgi	Betty L. Ravnik, CMKBD
Jerome Hankins, CKD	Robert Schaefer
Spencer Hinkle, CKD	Klaudia Spivey, CMKBD
Max Isley, CMKBD	Kelly Stewart, CMKBD
Mark Karas, CMKBD	Tom Trzcinski, CMKBD
Martha Kerr, CMKBD	Stephanie Witt, CMKBD

THANK YOU TO OUR SPONSORS

The National Kitchen & Bath Association recognizes with gratitude the following companies who generously helped to fund the creation of this industry resource.

PATRONS

www.americanwoodmark.com

www.kohler.com

iii

BENEFACTORS

www.monogram.com

www.subzero.com   www.wolfappliance.com

CONTRIBUTOR

www.groheamerica.com

SUPPORTERS

www.showhouse.moen.com

TOTO®

www.totousa.com

DONORS

Rev-A-Shelf | Viking Range Corp. | Whirlpool Corp.

About The National Kitchen & Bath Association

As the only non-profit trade association dedicated exclusively to the kitchen and bath industry, the National Kitchen & Bath Association (NKBA) is the leading source of information and education for all professionals in the field.

The NKBA's mission is to enhance member success and excellence, promote professionalism and ethical business practices, and provide leadership and direction for the kitchen and bath industry worldwide.

A non-profit trade association with more than 40,000 members in North America and overseas, it has provided valuable resources for industry professionals for more than 45 years. Its members are the finest professionals in the kitchen and bath industry.

The NKBA has pioneered innovative industry research, developed effective business management tools, and set groundbreaking design standards for safe, functional, and comfortable kitchens and baths.

The NKBA provides a unique, one-stop resource for professional reference materials, seminars and workshops, distance learning opportunities, marketing assistance, design competitions, consumer referrals, employment and internship availabilities, and opportunities to serve in leadership positions.

Recognized as the kitchen and bath industry's education and information leader, the NKBA provides development opportunities and continuing education for professionals of all levels of experience. More than 200 classes, as well as a certification program with three internationally recognized levels, help kitchen and bath professionals raise the bar for excellence.

For students entering the industry, the NKBA offers Accredited and Supported Programs which provide NKBA-approved curriculum at more than 60 learning institutions throughout the United States and Canada.

The NKBA helps members and other industry professionals stay on the cutting-edge of an ever-changing field through the Association's Kitchen & Bath Industry Show (KBIS®), one of the largest trade shows in the country.

The NKBA offers membership in 11 different industry segments: dealers, designers, manufacturers and suppliers, multi-branch retailers and home centers, decorative plumbing and hardware, manufacturer's representatives, builders and remodelers, installers, fabricators, cabinet shops, and distributors. For more information, visit NKBA.org.

The topic of project management is so important that an entire chapter in the NKBA book, *Kitchen & Bath Business Management* is devoted to this subject. The material in this book focuses on the kitchen and bath dealership owner's oversight responsibilities around project management— information valuable to the designer, as well.

Two other books provide an understanding of the construction and mechanical system details at the foundation of our industry. Becoming familiar with the information in the NKBA books *Residential Construction* and *Kitchen & Bath Systems* is an essential part of the designer's education.

Equally critical is appreciating the importance of proper project documentation. The NKBA book *Kitchen & Bath Drawing* covers the details of measuring the jobsite accurately, and then preparing all project drawings following accepted industry standards.

The NKBA Business Management Forms System

A business management tool created by the National Kitchen & Bath Association for its membership is an integral part of project management as well.

Seasoned, professional members of the National Kitchen & Bath Association invested countless hours sharing their expertise with the Association to assist in the creation of a Business Management Forms System. The resulting management tool contains a complete set of project documents and management forms that help the one-person design firm or large dealership produce projects efficiently and profitably.

A sample of each form, along with an explanation of its intended use, is included in appropriate sections throughout this book. Access to these business management forms is a benefit of NKBA membership.

Figure I.1 *The NKBA Business Management Forms System.*

1. **Lead System**
   Client Registration Card BMF1
   Prospective Client Record BMF2
   Company Lead Register.. BMF3
   Sales Consultant Lead Analysis............................... BMF4

2. **Pricing Tabulation Forms**
   Price Quotation BMF5
   Price Quotation with Cost Column BMF5A
   Contract Installer Agreement................................ BMF6
   Subcontractor Agreement..................................... BMF7

3. **Survey Forms**
   Kitchen Design Survey Form.................................. BMF8
   Bathroom Design Survey Form................................ BMF9

4. **Drawing Document**
   Plan Title Block BMF10

5. **Estimate Form**
   Estimate Form for Kitchen Design and Installation BMF11
   Estimate Form for Bathroom Design and Installation............. BMF12

6. **Specifications Form**
   Standard Specifications for Kitchen Design and Installation BMF13
   Standard Specifications for Bathroom Design & Installation....... BMF14

7. **Contracts**
   Standard Form of Agreement for Design and Consultation Services .. BMF15
   Design Fee/Retainer Estimate Sheet BMF16
   Standard Form of Agreement for Design and Installation .... BMF17 & BMF17A

8. **Change Orders**
   Change in Plans and Specifications........................... BMF18
   Change in Plans and Specifications with Cost Column BMF18A

9. **Job Progress Management**
   Job Progress Chart... BMF19
   Time Card BMF20
   Onsite Project Communication Form BMF21
   Project Pre-installation Conference Detail List.................. BMF22
   Project Production Start Checklist............................ BMF23
   Pre-Close-in Punchlist BMF24
   Final Inspection Before Punchlist with Client.................. BMF25

10. **Service Call System**
    Pre-Completion Conference Detail List BMF26
    Customer Complaint Form BMF27
    Industry Feedback Response Form BMF28

11. **Job Completion and Follow-up System**
    Completion Report... BMF29
    NKBA Limited Warranty..................................... BMF30
    NKBA Follow-up Letter BMF31
    NKBA Client Evaluation Form BMF32

CHAPTER 1: Attributes of a Successful Kitchen and Bath Designer

The successful kitchen and bath designer balances the artistry of design with the details and methodology of construction management with these goals in mind: creating a profitable project and a happy client.

Recently, NKBA surveyed homeowners who remodeled their kitchen or bath during the past year. Happily, 80% of the homeowners were somewhat or completely satisfied with the outcome of their remodel. The balance—20%—felt somewhat or completely dissatisfied with their project.

To insure your clients are in that 80% category, work towards developing the following skill sets:

THE NECESSARY SKILLS TO EXCEL IN THE BUSINESS OF DESIGN

The successful kitchen and bath designer knows design is a business.

Product Knowledge/Trend Watching

The successful designer represents a select group of products and is familiar with all the details of those products. The designer chooses which products to represent by conducting in-depth research. The successful designer further enhances their product knowledge by actively participating in training programs offered by supplier partners and manufacturers.

The successful designer keeps an eye out for emerging design trends and new product introductions and is capable of presenting up-to-date ideas to clients.

Design Ability

The successful designer studies the art and science of residential kitchen and bath design and consistently learns from peers, colleagues —even competitors—by participating in industry events and regularly reading major trade journals.

Attention to Technical Details

The successful designer understands that project profits and happy clients depend on the technical details of the design solution. A beautiful rendering is simply an artist's interpretation of the solution. Only detailed project documentation really explains the designer's concept. Successful designers either produce these documents themselves or collaborate with associate designers to insure all individuals responsible for transforming a drawing into reality understand their solution.

Sales Skills

The successful designer understands the power of persuasion and the importance good salesmanship plays in their success.

Team Building Talents

The successful designer realizes they are part of a team, and that each team member has a specific role to play in successfully producing a project. Sometimes, mix-ups occur when the individuals do not understand their roles. In our industry, the following titles describe various responsibilities:

- *Owner/Owner's Agent*: The client assumes all decision-making responsibilities or delegates them to an individual identified as their agent. The owner's agent may be the architect, designer, builder, business manager or even a relative. To insure a clear understanding of everyone's responsibility, you should provide a statement outlining the breadth and responsibility of your work if you will not be dealing directly with the homeowner.

- *Designer of Record*: The designer of record is the professional who the client originally retains. The designer of record may be an interior designer, who then invites a kitchen specialist to collaborate on the project. Alternatively, the kitchen firm's designer, who the client was referred to or who met the client in the showroom, is the designer of record. This individual is normally the member of the project team who is accountable to the client.

- *Co-Designer*: The co-designer can be an assistant to the designer of record, an individual who is contributing to the overall project, or collaborating with the designer of record. The title co-designer can apply to an individual who focuses on one aspect of the project, while the designer of record takes a holistic approach to the project, considering it in its totality.

- *Design Associate/Assistant*: A team member hired by the kitchen/bath designer to assist in the planning process or in the project management. Clearly communicate the breadth of responsibility of such an associate to the team.

- *Production Manager*: This term applies to an individual who assumes management of an entire project. This person is not working with tools (and, in fact, may not even be a tradesperson) but whose main responsibility is to manage the flow of work, coordinate the trades, and bring the project to completion. This position is typical in commercial work and in large-scale residential construction.

- *Site Superintendent*: This refers to an individual who supervises an entire site, usually containing more than one home, such as a new home development (or building in multi-story structures). "Supers" are on the site to supervise and coordinate. On some projects, they spend a large amount of time scheduling so that the subs work to maximum efficiency. In high-rise living environments, the "super" is there to oversee the work and to insure completion within the building covenants.

- *Project Manager*: This is the term for an individual who is based offsite and who travels from jobsite to jobsite. Project managers can have responsibility for more than one job in different locales and give onsite direction—often specific instruction on the work for that day. A project manager orders material and schedules subs, etc. The owner of a remodeling company often plays this role until the jobs become too numerous to handle.

- *Lead Installer (Carpenter)*: This term refers to a tradesperson who assumes management responsibility while continuing to work with their tools on the job. These jobs are typically smaller in nature than the jobs a project manager would manage—anywhere from $10,000 to as high as $500,000.

- *Journeyman Installer (Carpenter)*: An individual who has reached journeyman status through an examination and/or testing function as part of a trade association or labor union. The term "journeyman" is defined as: "*(1) a worker who has learned a trade and works for another person, usually by the day; (2) an experienced, reliable worker or performer especially as distinguished from one who is brilliant or colorful.*"

For a firm that does not retain union labor, the term "journeyman installer" and/or "journeyman carpenter" often applies to the most senior member of the installation team who has demonstrated capability through their years of service.

- *Apprentice Installer (Carpenter)*: The term "apprentice" is defined as: *"(1a) one bound by indenture to serve another for a prescribed period with a view to learning an art or trade; (1b) one who is learning by practical experience under skilled workers a trade, art, or calling; (2) an inexperienced person."* Therefore, an apprentice installer or apprentice carpenter is learning a trade from installers participating in an organized union, trade guild or trade association. For a firm that does employ union labor, the term "apprentice" is used to designate an individual who is learning the trade.

- *Helper*: The term "helper" is slang, used in the construction industry to designate an individual who is just entering the field, and who assists in all activities. The helper allows the apprentice and/or journeyman to complete tasks in the most efficient way. For example, the helper might be in charge of unpacking materials, moving product in and out of the room, daily sweeping chores, and maintaining the truck in a neat and orderly fashion.

Construction Knowledge

The successful designer realize they cannot propose a design solution unless it is grounded in a keen understanding of construction systems used in North America, including the mechanical systems found in older dwellings, as well as current systems, building regulations/codes and the permitting process.

Appreciate the Importance of Customer Service

The successful designer is aware that it is often difficult for a consumer to understand a new construction or a renovation project. Successful designers realize that customer service revolves around communication.

- Many consumers have a hard time visualizing floor plan and elevation drawings. Experienced designers use artistic renderings, CAD interactive drawings or a portfolio (picture book) of images to help explain a proposed design solution to the consumer.

Project Purchases

The design firm representative (it may be the designer or a separate purchasing department) places all orders for the materials. These materials will be delivered directly to the jobsite or to the firm's staging area.

The "Good Neighbor" Program

Successful firms work hard to avoid disrupting the neighborhood during renovation projects. Typically, this is not a concern in new construction. (See *Kitchen & Bath Business Management*, Chapter 11.)

The Delivery, Installation and Punchlist Process

Materials are delivered and installed. Debris is removed, the jobsite cleaned and the punchlist is completed.

After-sale/Installation Service

Wise designers stay in touch with the consumer after the project is completed to protect their referral business.

Cost Analysis

Make a final comparison between the estimated costs of the project used as the basis for the contract and the actual costs incurred. This allows the firm to engage in continuous process improvement so they manage all jobs better.

TIME MANAGEMENT

The successful designer is an expert in time management.

There have been books written on how to effectively manage time. Experts all seem to agree that a system needs to be in place to guide you and all other individuals involved in a new construction or renovation project from beginning to completion.

The National Kitchen & Bath Association has developed a "Business Management Forms System" (BMFS), referenced in the introduction of this book, which will help you organize your design, estimating and project management process, and help you manage your time much more efficiently by providing you the forms, checklists and other information needed to manage a project from beginning to end expeditiously.

The Lead System

Either the individual designer or the design firm keeps track of leads. Individual designers follow up on these leads.

The NKBA Business Management Forms System contains four forms to help designers keep track of leads.

1. Client Registration Card, BMF1
2. Prospective Client Record, BMF2
3. Company Lead Register, BMF3
4. Sales Consultant Lead Analysis, BMF4

Use the Lead System as the basis for evaluating marketing and sales information and to determine the number of leads generated by marketing activities in order to develop marketing cost per lead, by source. Use it to determine the quality of a lead by comparing source/average sales or source/percentage of closes. The system also provides a management tool for the sales manager and a cash flow indicator for the business manager.

The **Lead System** forms will provide:

1. A record of prospective clients' contact and project information.
2. Information for the sales consultant.
3. Information about the lead source.
4. A record of project sales activity.
5. Statistical information for salesperson performance review.

Use the **Client Registration Card** form at home shows, traveling displays, group consumer meetings, or in any other situation where adequate time cannot be spent with a prospect. This record can be used to set up appointments for a showroom visit.

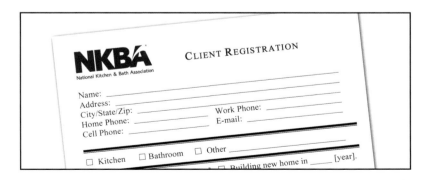

Figure 1.1 *The NKBA Client Registration Card.*

THE DESIGN SURVEY FORMS

The Design Survey Form will provide:

1. Design information relative to the personal needs and desires of the client.

2. A complete listing of equipment and materials.

3. Construction information regarding the physical restrictions of the project.

4. Information to develop a budget for the project.

5. Project contact information.

The client completes the Design Survey Form either before a scheduled appointment or with the designer during a showroom/home visit. Exercise care to consider all aspects of the project. Digital photography is encouraged. Use the information indicated on the Design Survey Form to set the criteria for the designer.

File the completed Design Survey Form in the job folder of the individual client. Review the Design Survey Form with the client during the presentation session.

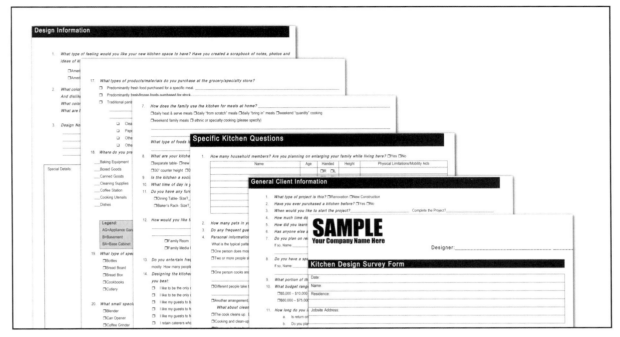

Figure 1.5 *The NKBA Kitchen Design Survey Forms.*

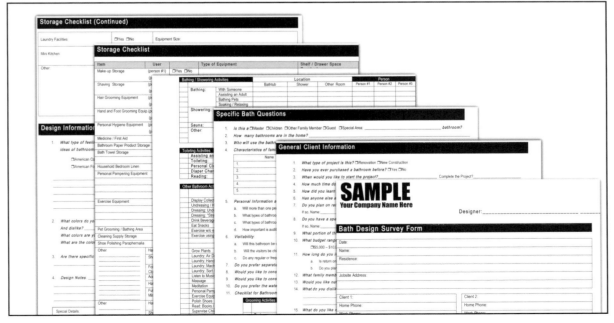

Figure 1.6 *The NKBA Bathroom Design Survey Forms.*

The **Agreements** consist of two forms:

1. Contract Installer Agreement, BMF6

2. Subcontractor Agreement, BMF7

The Agreement forms provide an organized way to detail exactly what work the contractor/subcontractor will be completing at the jobsite, what the payment schedule will be for the work, what documentation the firm has supplied the contractor/subcontractor to guide them in the preparation of the estimate, and the general conditions established by the design business, which must be adhered to by contractors/subcontractors on the jobsite.

Figure 1.8 *The NKBA Contract Installer Agreement.*

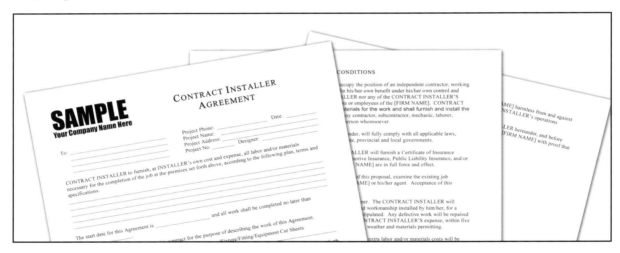

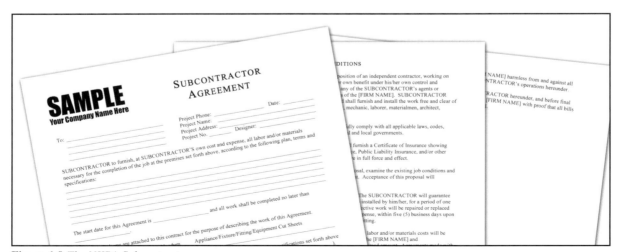

Figure 1.9 *The NKBA Subcontractor Agreement.*

Material Selection and Specification

Design firms follow different business models for material selections. For example, some design firms offer a turnkey service, providing all components necessary to complete the project and charging fees to cover the time and expense of assisting the consumer with all their selections. Other firms focus on cabinets, countertops and appliances. Regardless of the type of business model you use, materials need to be selected or allowances provided.

Additionally, the designer and the firm should be working within a system that includes a design retainer. Following such a format saves a lot of wasted time. The NKBA Business Management Forms System includes a detailed overview of types of design fee systems.

THE STANDARD FORM OF AGREEMENT FOR DESIGN AND CONSULTATION SERVICES

There are many ways kitchen and bath dealerships offer design services to their clients. Additionally, the design process for a kitchen or bath normally includes four different steps, which need to be factored into the design fee system employed by the firm. In some cases, different phases of the project are better planned with different fee structures. Therefore, the National Kitchen & Bath Association does not recommend one standard form for design and consultation services. However, NKBA does offers a series of questions the dealership answers to help to develop a personalized Standard Form of Agreement for Design and Consultation Services.

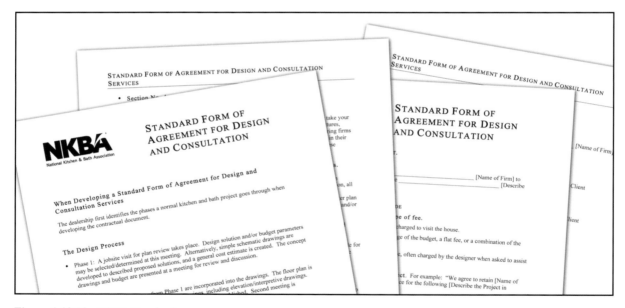

Figure 1.10 *The NKBA Standard Form For Design and Consultation Services.*

STANDARD FORM OF AGREEMENT FOR DESIGN AND INSTALLATION AND CHANGE ORDER SYSTEM

A legally binding agreement, or contract, that clearly defines what products, materials and services will be supplied by the kitchen specialist, the owner or the owner's agent is a key step in the project documentation procedure. Project information (without selling price information) from the contract is often included as part of the project documents used by the tradespeople on the jobsite.

The NKBA Business Management Forms System also includes a Standard Form of Agreement, as well as a Change Order Form.

THE STANDARD FORM OF AGREEMENT FOR DESIGN AND INSTALLATION, BMF17 AND BMF17A.

The National Kitchen & Bath Association publishes the Standard Form of Agreement for Design and Installation (BMF17 and BMF17A). This Standard Form of Agreement provides information and general advice, which may have substantial legal consequences. The laws of the various states/provinces are different and may impose particular limitations on the use of this agreement or require that additional provisions be included in order to make the agreement binding and enforceable. You should not use this agreement unless you obtain specific legal advice geared to your specific situation and the state/province in which you are located. No published material or contract is a substitute for personalized advice from a knowledgeable attorney licensed to practice in your state/province. The National Kitchen & Bath Association makes no representation or warranty that the Standard Form of Agreement is appropriate for your particular use or valid and enforceable in your state/province.

Figure 1.11 The NKBA Standard Form of Agreement for Design and Installation.

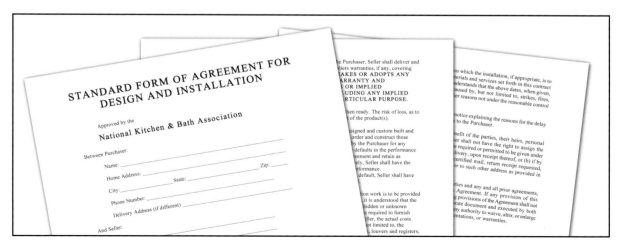

THE CHANGE ORDER SYSTEM

The Change Order System is comprised of two similar forms:

1. Change in Plans and Specifications, BMF18

2. Change in Plans and Specifications with Cost Column,
   BMF18A

Complete the Change Order whenever the client requests changes in the contract, specifications and/or plans of the project.

The changes should be explicit and priced in order to indicate any credit or additional charges for the changes.

All parties signing the original contract for the project are required to sign the Change in Plans and Specifications form.

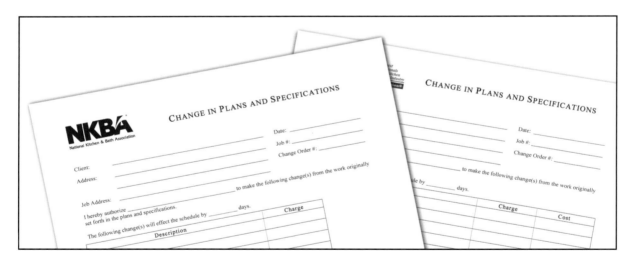

Figure 1.12 *The NKBA Change in Plans and Specifications Forms*

Project Management

Managing the project efficiently means everybody wins. NKBA provides an entire series of forms to assist you in managing the project. Following is a listing of these forms, as well as a sample.

THE JOB PROGRESS MANAGEMENT FORMS

The Job Progress Management System is comprised of seven separate forms:

1. Job Progress Chart, BMF19

2. Time Card, BMF20

3. Onsite Project Communication, BMF21

4. Project Pre-installation Conference Detail List, BMF22

5. Project Production Start Checklist, BMF23

6. Pre-Close-in Punchlist, BMF24

7. Final Inspection Before Punchlist with Client, BMF25

The Job Progress Management Forms will provide:

1. An easy review of the job and the status of each section.

2. A ready instrument for scheduling of the job as it progresses.

3. An outline of all information to review before installation begins.

4. An outline of all information and materials the production department should receive before work begins on the project.

5. An organized way to communicate with various individuals on the jobsite.

6. A systematic way to inspect the jobsite and specific check points to verify adherence to plan details and to gather information about corrective, add-on or warranty work required to complete the project.

Keep the Job Progress Management Forms inside the job folder or jobsite binder for easy access.

The expeditor or individual responsible for ordering labor, product and/or material should complete the **Job Progress Chart** as the information is received or scheduled, generally on a daily basis.

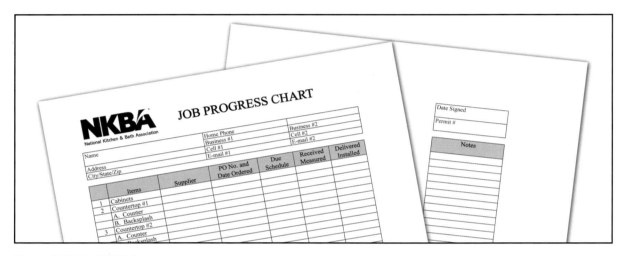

Figure 1.13 *The NKBA Progress Chart.*

Jobsite personnel use the **time card** to note the time required to complete tasks on an individual project. This information is useful when reviewing the project to determine the overall time required per general category of work performed. A time card evaluation may also assist the designer when discussing final billing with contractors, subcontractors or the client.

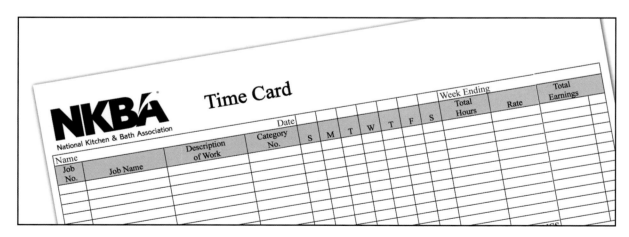

Figure 1.14 *The NKBA Time Card.*

The **Onsite Job Communication Form** provides a simple way to manage written communications. Far better than notes written on the wall by the phone, or Post It notes left on a window, the form gives an individual a clear format to direct a question or message to a colleague, the designer, another trade or the client and to receive a written message in response.

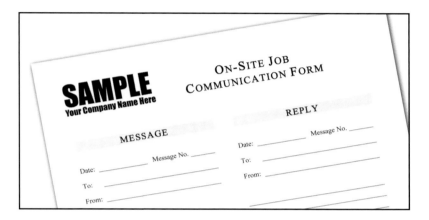

Figure 1.15 *The NKBA Onsite Job Communication Form.*

The **Project Pre-installation Conference Detail List** is a useful management tool if the installation is the responsibility of the design firm.

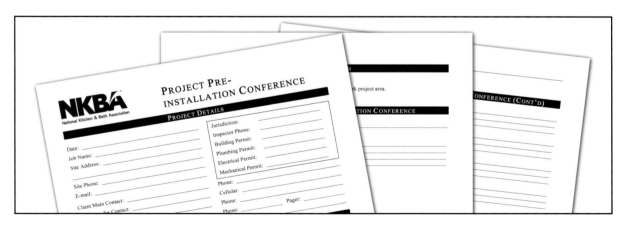

Figure 1.16 *The NKBA Project Pre-installation Conference Detail List.*

The **Project Production Start Checklist** is used as a guide before the project starts. It is also useful if the designer transfers installation responsibility to someone else.

Figure 1.17 *The NKBA Project Production Start Checklist.*

The **Pre-close-in Punchlist** is a checklist that gives the lead installer, project manager or designer responsible for the installation an opportunity to review the electrical, plumbing, HVAC and framing work completed to-date in preparation for a building department inspection. This review also allows the designer of record or their representative to check all mechanical, HVAC and framing work completed to-date compared to the project documents, insuring that once the equipment arrives and installation begins all preparatory work will be properly positioned, complete and to code.

Figure 1.18 *The NKBA Pre-close-in Punchlist.*

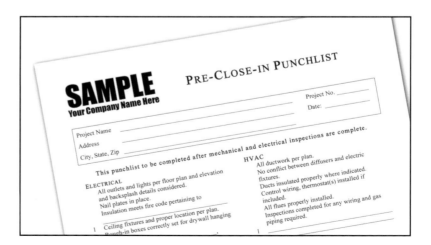

The **Final Inspection Before Punchlist with Client Review** is a check sheet that allows the lead installer, project manager or designer responsible for project supervision to review the various equipment categories of the project, insuring that the fit and finish of these materials are correct and proper and, therefore, ready to review with the owner and/or owner's agent. Such a checklist is an excellent way to make sure a project is closely reviewed by the responsible representatives of the design firm, with notations for corrective or replacement work made before the project is reviewed with the consumer.

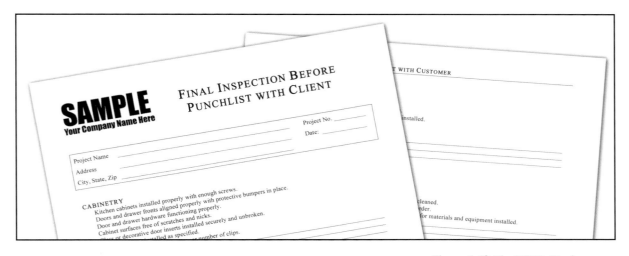

Figure 1.19 *The NKBA Final Inspection Before Punchlist with Client form.*

Charging Design Fees for Large Projects

Kitchen & Bath Business Management discusses different design fee systems. For unusually large projects, a three-tier design system, which begins with a fee to cover the conceptual plans, followed by a project documentation fee and concluding with a selection service fee, is a good way to make sure you are compensated for this type of time-consuming project.

Estimating Labor and Materials for Large Projects

Seasoned professionals accustomed to working on large projects advise that money is often lost in labor miscalculations on large, complex projects. Insist on firm proposals or estimates with specific times identified for project segments from subcontractors, or "best guess" guidelines from your internal team.

Allow Enough Time to Manage These Projects

Oftentimes, large or complex projects require an extensive amount of attention by the designer of record. Jobsite visits, meetings with other allied professionals and the selection process might take far more time than the professional normally sets aside for a simple kitchen and/or bath project. It is critical that the designer allow enough time for these extra responsibilities within their normal workday so they can service the owner and/or owner's agent on the large project without losing the needed momentum of new business.

Staging Large Projects

Carefully plot the production or the project's staging, allowing you to work on this large project in tandem with (rather than in place of) your current installations underway, and without limiting your ability to continue prospecting for new clients.

Know Who Is On the Design Team For a Large Project

It is critical to know the entire group of professionals who will be working on a large project and exactly what your responsibilities are within that team. Business managers also stress how important it is you maintain control over your portion of the project. Sometimes, an influential client can intimidate a designer, or a well-known design professional can persuasively push the kitchen specialist into a product specification or design detail that does not reflect good planning. Both of these situations can lead to profit slippage.

Charge Enough

Some designers think a larger job can carry a smaller margin. Just the reverse is true. A large, time-consuming project that does not generate the company's projected profit margin possible from a series of smaller projects should be avoided. Savvy, skilled designers urge you to charge MORE—not less—for these large projects.

CHAPTER 2: Client Relationships

MANAGING THE DESIGN AND INSTALLATION PROCESS

Managing the client's expectations means preparing the client for the tough realities of remodeling. Begin by explaining what's required for a job to run smoothly, with a focus on your ability to follow through on your promises. In this time of televised home make-overs and starry-eyed homeowners, it is a strategy that can be invaluable for minimizing the surprises and setbacks that can eat time, burn money and turn relationships toxic.

The Role of the Designer

There are a variety of successful "job descriptions" for designers in our industry.

1. **The designer is responsible for all aspects of the planning process.**

   In this business model, the designer is solely responsible for client contact in the showroom, during the planning process (in the showroom or on the jobsite), estimating the cost of the project, ordering the material and monitoring material delivery. If the firm installs product, the designer is also the project liaison: orchestrating site preparation, material delivery and installation.

2. **The designer works with an in-house or out-sourced drafting department and transfers project management responsibility to a production manager.**

   In this business model, the designer's primary responsibility is client contact and creating concept design solutions. The designer meets with the client in the showroom and/or in the home, and then creates the concept solution. These concept sketches are then transferred to an in-house or out-sourced design department who interfaces with the designer of record and creates the working drawings and completes estimating. Once the project is sold, the design department may also be responsible for ordering material. The project is then "handed off" to a production manager, who assumes responsibility for jobsite management and serves as liaison between the designer, the client and the installation team.

3. The designer works with a design associate during the planning process.

In this business model, there is a team of two individuals—the designer of record and a design associate. The design associate may interface with other people within the design firm, or may serve as the drawing source. Typically, the design associate is responsible for assisting the client in surface selections, securing estimates and proposals from subcontractors or contract installers, and preparing jobsite workbook materials. In some organizations, the design associate has more project management responsibility: once again, allowing the senior designer to focus on design and selling, as opposed to project management or the technical details associated with the ordering process. Alternatively, installation may be supervised by the designer and design associate as detailed under No. 1, or the project may be transferred to a production manager as outlined in No. 2.

Establishing Project Management Responsibility

Most kitchen and bathroom installations require more than just a carpentry specialist. Electricians, plumbers, tile setters and others are part of the installation team. Contracting and scheduling with these additional craftspeople can be challenging.

Understanding who does what can also be surprising—for example, just because a plumber is there to install the sink does not mean he cuts the hole in the countertop to put the sink in. The electrician might arrive to connect the oven. However, they expect an installer to be onsite to place the oven in the cabinet opening.

The key issue in this relationship is:

Who is accountable to the client, and who is paying whom?

- The installer/contractor works directly for the client and the designer is an advisor. The client signs a contract with the installer/contractor and pays him/her directly.

  The advantage to this type of arrangement is that jobsite management does not consume the designer's time. However, this type of arrangement means the designer assumes that the installer/contractor will clearly understand the plans and execute them according to the designer's intent. This scenario is rarely the most successful.

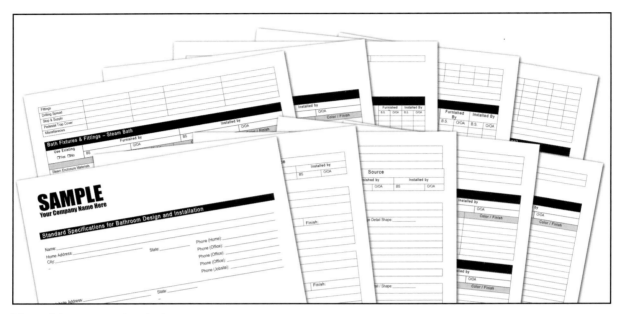

Figure 2.2 *The NKBA Standard Specifications for Bathroom Design and Installation.*

How to Handle Changes Once the Job Begins

Ideally, the project specifications and project documentation will detail all materials and all installation activities needed to complete a project. However—in the real world—construction surprises may occur once the demolition stage starts and clients may change their minds or request additional work once the project starts. Document any change in the original project specifications with a change order that includes all appropriate pricing information. Have all change orders signed by the owner or owner's agent.

Figure 2.3 *The NKBA Change in Plans and Specifications Form*

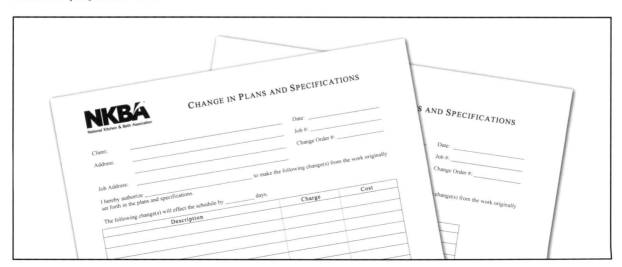

Ask any seasoned pro and they will probably have a "horror story" from their past where they did not document changes and the client was surprised—perhaps even outraged—when the final bill was presented with the additional charges. In most cases, some type of negotiation followed, and the designer was never fully compensated for the changes requested by the owner. All because the changes were not documented step-by-step in a change order.

The purpose of a change order is to amend the original project specifications and documentation. Initiate a change order whenever a client requests goods or services outside those specified in the original proposal, or when additional work must be performed because of the discovery of unknown, hidden construction contingencies. The installer, project manager and/or designer can execute the change order, using an established format. Execute the change order and have it approved by the client in writing or via e-mail before the work is completed. Part of the change order process is to make sure a copy is filed with the design firm's accounting department so these changes are duly recorded and integrated into the payment schedule.

In new construction, the most profitable part of the sale for the builder or general contractor may be the "upgrades" or "changes" the homeowner requests. In the kitchen and bath design business this is not the case. However, it is not uncommon for a change order item to carry a larger markup percentage than the full project markup because of the additional time it will take to execute the change, as well as the additional risk/responsibility assumed by the designer or design firm as they "think through the entire project" to identify what parts of the project this change order impacts.

Whatever the markup factor is, most professionals agree that a deposit on the estimated work or the agreed-to price listed on the change order should be collected at the time of change order signing so the outstanding final payment never exceeds the final payment percentage established by the firm's business managers.

Change orders are so important that some firms will refuse to pay the designer's commission, or the additional charges listed on a subcontractor or contract installer's bill if the proper change order process has not been followed.

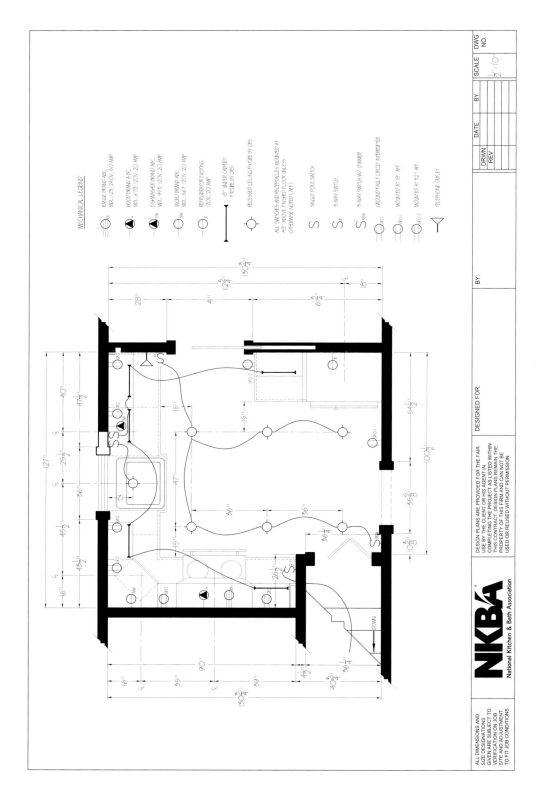

Figure 2.5 Kitchen mechanical plan.
(Concept by Mary Galloway, CKD – Alexandria, Virginia)

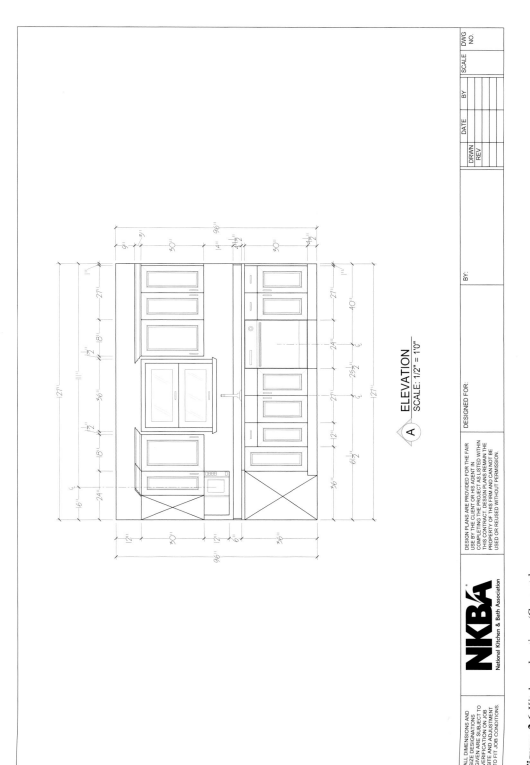

Figure 2.6 Kitchen elevation. (Concept by Mary Galloway, CKD – Alexandria, Virginia)

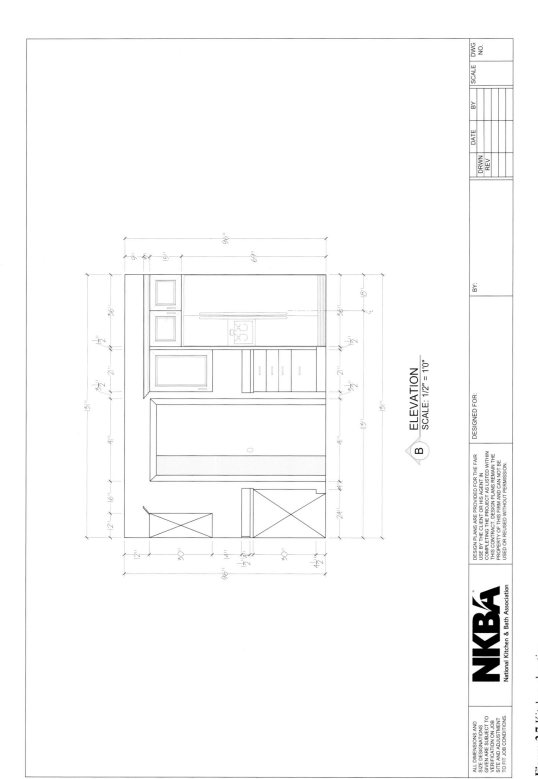

Figure 2.7 Kitchen elevation.
(Concept by Mary Galloway, CKD –
Alexandria, Virginia)

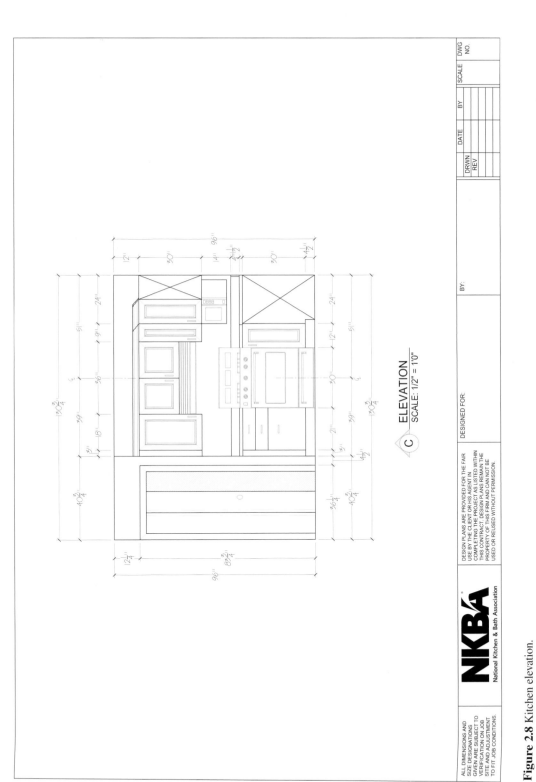

ELEVATION
SCALE: 1/2" = 1'0"

Figure 2.8 Kitchen elevation.
(Concept by Mary Galloway, CKD –
Alexandria, Virginia)

Managing the Jobsite

It is on the jobsite that the tough realities of remodeling are, literally, driven home to the client, and where people management skills are critical to maintaining client relationships.

It is the responsibility of the project manager to prepare the client for the inevitable mess, and up to the installation team to minimize and contain as much of this disruption as possible. A thorough pre-construction meeting sets the stage for a successful project and helps determine how clients live and what precautions you should take in and around their home.

Clearly define the actual work zone so the client, designer and all installation professionals onsite know what areas are off-limits as well as what spaces are accessible to crew members.

TIPS FROM THE MASTERS

Here are some questions to ask during the pre-construction meeting:

What hours can we work?

What days can we work?

What areas of the home do we need special permission to enter?

Where is your security alarm system?

Can we use a lockbox system during your project?

If the home has wireless connectivity, may we have access to your wireless network? If not, is there a high-speed Internet line available to us in the work zone?

Regarding children: what is their daily schedule, who is responsible for them if they return home when parents are working?

Are there any pet considerations?

Are there any neighbor concerns?

Where can we drop/store deliveries, notably the cabinets and/or crated, oversized bathroom fixtures?

What do you want to salvage from demolition, and where do you want it stored?

Where can we place the trash?

Where can we place the portable toilet? (Or, which of your bathrooms can we use?)

Do you have snow removal service? How will plowing patterns affect the trash or storage areas?

Where can we park our vehicles?

Where can we post company signs?

Where are your utilities (gas, electric, septic, communications)?

What furniture or shrubbery needs to be moved?

What hours can we call you, and what numbers should we use (home, work, cell, other)?

Can we install a phone/fax line for the duration of the project?

How often do you want us to meet with/contact you?

Do you understand our request that no family members or other unauthorized individuals spend time in the work zone, and that all communication is best maintained between the designer or our appointed responsible project manager and the owner or your representative?

What can we do to make the project more enjoyable for you?

The reality of any renovation is that air-borne dust particulates will filter throughout the house, there is trash that must be disposed of and—as hard as everyone tries—the jobsite can look disheveled. Here are some recommendations for protecting the jobsite.

- Drop cloths should always be used from the agreed-to entry to the construction site.

- Protective floor covering, covers for bathtubs, drapes to cover cabinets and plywood/cardboard coverings for finished countertops should always be in-place so no new material becomes a landing surface for tools.

- See-through plastic sheeting or specially designed dust barriers for doorways, passageways and room dividers are a must. Door systems specifically designed with zipper closure systems are much better than haphazardly taped sheets of plastic.

- The client must move all of their belongings to a temporary storage area that does not interfere with the staging area, the trash collection area, or the work site.

- Where and how trash will be collected is an important decision. If a trash container is ordered, where will it be placed? And are there any community regulations about its location on the property?

- Who is responsible for moving and storing any precious possessions (the grand piano or art collection) adjacent to the kitchen or bath project?

- Where will a temporary kitchen, or closet, be set up? Successful designers often provide special equipment for their clients, such as:

  1. Rolling hanging racks to create temporary closets in adjacent spaces when master bath suites/closets are worked on.

  2. Portable tables, microwave oven and "on-loan" freestanding refrigerator to assist the client in setting up a temporary kitchen.

  3. Plastic bins (clear preferably) for the client to store their kitchen or laundry/cleaning equipment.

Close contact with your client during the installation process is a key to success.

The NKBA Business Management Forms System includes a document to help you leave messages or questions at the jobsite.

Figure 2.9 *The NKBA Onsite Job Communication Form.*

TIPS FROM THE MASTERS

Seasoned professionals suggest you pay close attention to the client's state of mind and that you are timely and accurate in your responses to any calls or questions:

Never start the project without the jobsite workbook onsite. Never let this book leave the jobsite.

Exchange cell numbers or beeper numbers. Use these devices and respond to messages as soon as possible.

Make sure you are open and direct in your communication. Make sure the other person understands your communication.

Direct questions or comments to the appropriate person. All too often, helpers on the jobsite will be asked a question and will respond to an area outside of their responsibility. Or, an installer will make a suggestion to the client when it should have been made to the designer or project manager.

Communicate delays or problems to the owner or the owner's agent as soon as possible. Never leave the client hanging. Tim Faller of Field Training Services (www.leadcarpenter.com) reminds us to listen to the words—but watch the body language as well:

> "Many of us get into trouble by focusing on the words a client says, and not how they say them. Even if they say, 'This is turning into a beautiful project,' is there something bothering the client? When the tone and body language conflicts with the words, ask questions for clarification. Look the client in the eye, speak directly, convey control, authority and confidence. Remember, if the client feels these are lacking—life on that project could become miserable for everyone."

Do not spend a lot of time making apologies. If and when the inevitable mistake happens just fix it. No matter what the reason (excuse), it will sound complicated to the consumer and they don't care. They just want to know what does the mistake mean to the job progress: will the installation finish be delayed a month or two days?

Managing the Project Installation Forecast (Schedule)

Many designers and/or production managers are fearful of committing themselves to specific dates for the project schedule—and for good reason. To the consumer one of the most frustrating elements of a project is the time it takes to complete the work. There are weather concerns, economic concerns, custom materials that need to be ordered, etc.

Mark Richardson, president of Case Design/Remodeling and Case Handyman Services in Bethesda, Maryland, suggests using the word "forecast" (rather than "schedule") might help everyone understand the variable nature of the installation process.

Simply changing the language will not solve timing problems—but, by providing a project forecast, you paint a more accurate picture for the client.

Regardless of what you call it, to successfully manage an installation, create a timeline. There are many excellent computer programs and systems available for this purpose.

On page 50 is an example of one system that plots the number of days it will take to accomplish the installation of a project. PLEASE NOTE: THERE ARE TWO FREE DAYS PLANNED INTO THE PROCESS.

In addition to the daily activity forecast or schedule, the client must clearly understand:

- There will not be someone on the jobsite every day from 8:00 a.m. to 5:00 p.m. The nature of construction means some free days (where no work takes place) are part of the process.

- The extended lead time between stone countertop templating and installation is the norm across North America.

- The payment schedule is part of the project forecast. Some punchlist items, necessitating a separate jobsite work visit after "substantial completion" are to be expected.

PROJECT SCHEDULE

Project: _____

Calendar Period: _____

Page _____ of _____

Description Of Work	M 23	T 24	W 25	T 26	F 27	M 30	T 31	W 1	T 2	F 3	M 6	T 7	W 8	T 9	F 10	M 13	T 14	W 15	T 16	F 17	M 20	T 21	W 22	T 23	F 24	M 27	T 28	W 1	T 2	F 3	M 6	T 7	W 8	T 9	F 10
	Wk1 (January)					Wk2					Wk3 (February)					Wk4					Wk5					Wk6					Wk7 (March)				
1 Deliver Cabinets/2nd Payment Due	x																																		
2 Remove Cabinets/Tops		x	x																																
3 Lay Out Kitchen On Floor				x																															
4 Rough Wiring				x	x																														
5 Rough Plumbing						x	x	x																											
6 Building Dept. Inspection									x	x																									
7 Patch Walls											x	x																							
8 Free Day/Clean Jobsite													x																						
9 Install Cabinets														x	x	x																			
10 Inspect With Client																	x																		
11 Template Granite																		x																	
12 Paint																	x	x	x	x															
13 Lay Vinyl Flooring																					x														
14 Install Moulding/Set Appliances																						x	x												
15 Free Days/Contingent Time																								x	x	x									
16 Install Granite																												x							
17 Trim-out Electrical																													x						
18 Hook-up Plumbing																														x					
19 Inspect With Client/3rd Payment Due																														x					
20 Touch-up Paint																															x				
21 Complete Punchlist																																x			
22 Clean Jobsite																																	x		

x = Projected

Figure 2.10 *An Example of a Project Schedule Chart.*

Creating realistic product expectations begins the first time the design professional meets the client. During every step of the planning process, the client must be informed about material and equipment limitations, as well as the proper sequence of the selection process.

It is equally important for the client to appreciate how the realities of the construction process and hand crafted precision, as well as the natural movement of wood, affect the details of the design. The following information will help you to avoid common oversights often made when presenting the details of the project to the owner or the owner's agent.

- Clients need to know how impactful the appliance specifications are on the cabinetry order.

- Clients need to understand that wood characteristics are very different from wood defects—and that wood characteristics are magnified under a natural finish.

- Clients need to know that change orders can result in increased costs above and beyond the expected expense.

Some firms use waivers: a form the client signs when a decision they make does not coincide with the designer's best judgment. For example—if the appliances are not selected before the cabinet order is placed, a waiver must be signed by the client stating that placing an order for cabinetry prior to the confirmation of appliance selections can lead to delays if changes are made. Similarly, firms use a waiver if the client supplies the appliances. Waivers are also often used when clients select a natural finish on natural wood cabinet doors.

About the Fit (Relationship Between Adjacent Materials and Equipment)

In both new construction and renovation work, the consumer needs to understand that the building envelope may not be level, plumb or square. Therefore, cabinet reveals and scribing fillers must be part of the cabinet plan.

A Definition of a Level Surface: A surface without bends, curves, or irregularities. Normally refers to a horizontal surface.

Figure 2.11 *An example of an out-of-level floor.*

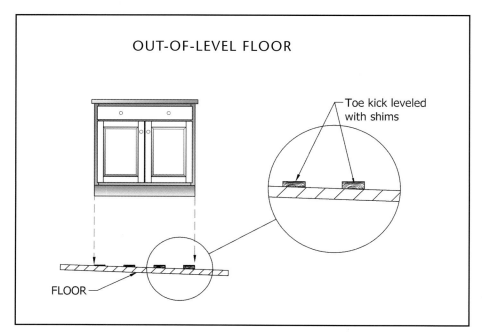

OUT-OF-LEVEL FLOOR

Toe kick leveled with shims

FLOOR

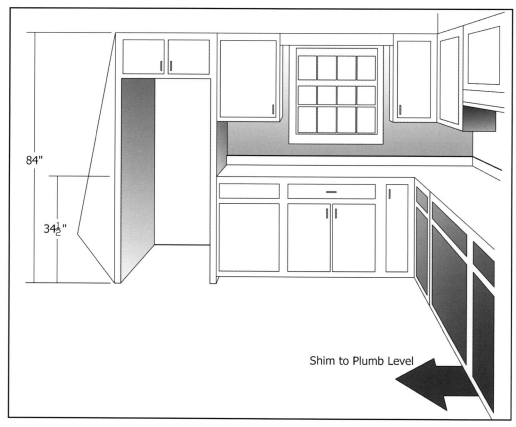

84"

34½"

Shim to Plumb Level

A Definition of a Plumb Surface: Perfectly straight. Normally refers to a vertical surface.

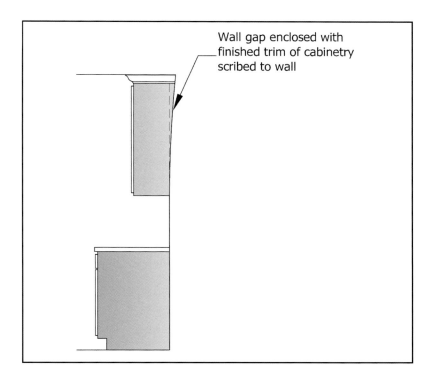

Wall gap enclosed with finished trim of cabinetry scribed to wall

Figure 2.12 *An example of an out-of-plumb wall.*

A Definition of a Square Corner: Two surfaces connecting at 90 degrees (a right angle) with no bends, curves or irregularities in either surface as it radiates out from the corner.

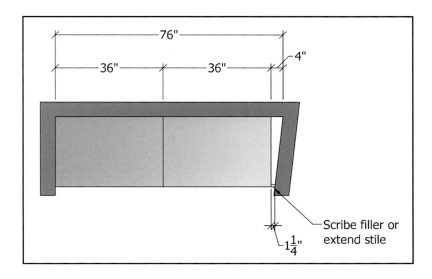

76"

36" 36" 4"

Scribe filler or extend stile

$1\frac{1}{4}$"

Figure 2.13 *An example of an out-of-square corner.*

The Impact of an Imperfect Room on the Cabinet Layout

FITTING CABINETS BETWEEN WALLS

Cabinets must be installed plumb and level—even in rooms that are not plumb, level and square. This becomes troublesome if cabinets are installed between two walls. Accentuating the problem is the fact that computer-generated design programs always assume the room is level and plumb and, therefore, will attempt to fit exact sized cabinetry in an opening.

For example, experienced designers never place two 36-inch wide cabinets in a 72-inch wide area. When the cabinets are leveled in an enclosure with walls out-of-plumb, the two 36-inch cabinets will not fit because the 72-inch space only exists along the back wall, not along the face of the cabinets 24 inches to 25 inches in front of that wall surface.

Extended stiles on framed cabinetry or separate fillers (sometimes called "scribes") are always used when cabinets are fit between walls to provide room for jobsite adjustment.

Figure 2.14 *Diagram of an out-of-plumb wall with cabinets using a scribing method or extended stile.*

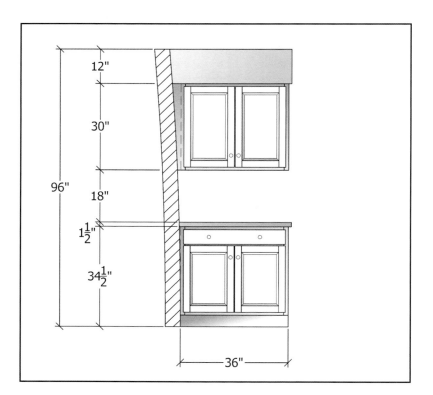

Scribing also takes place if cabinets extend to the ceiling.

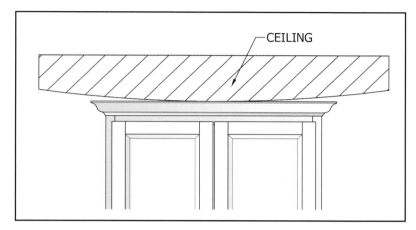

Figure 2.15 *Diagram of an out-of-level ceiling.*

THE FIT BETWEEN CABINETS

There is less fit flexibility in a full overlay cabinet because the door covers the entire case, while in a framed cabinet there is an extended frame that gives the installer more room to adjust cabinet sizing.

However, regardless of the case configuration, cabinets at right angles to one another, cabinets at right angles to an appliance on the return run, angled or diagonal cabinets in corners, or cabinets that are less in depth than adjacent units with crown moulding attached all require scribing space. Clients must appreciate why these scribes are used and what the visual reality is of a crown moulding scribed to the ceiling.

Figure 2.16 *Diagram of base and wall cabinets butting one another in a 90 degree corner.*

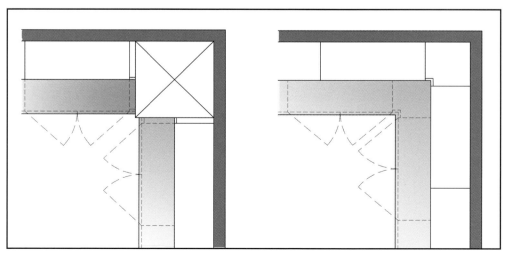

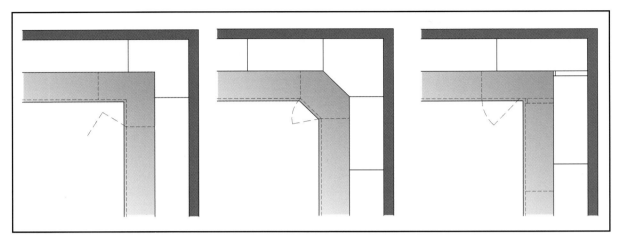

Figure 2.17 *Diagram of base and wall special purpose corner cabinet arrangements.*

Figure 2.18 *Diagram of full overlay cabinets at right angles to a cooking appliance with handles.*

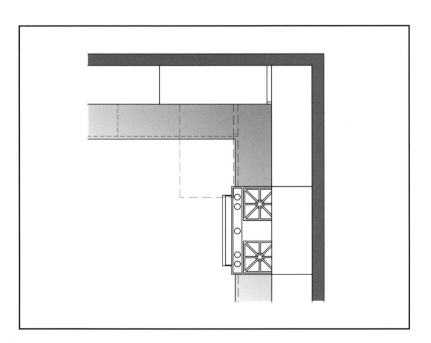

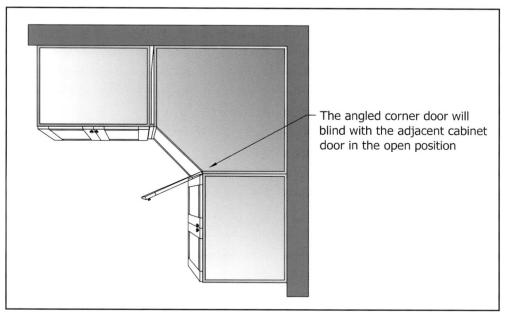

The angled corner door will blind with the adjacent cabinet door in the open position

Figure 2.19 *Diagram of a typical diagonal wall cabinet installation without required fillers.*

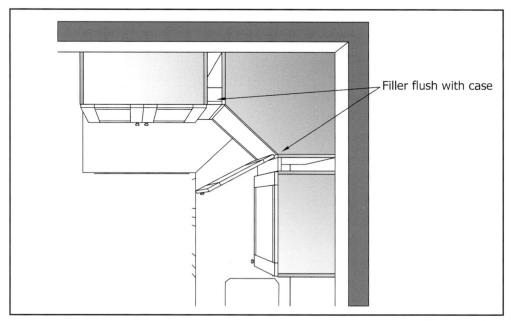

Filler flush with case

Figure 2.20 *Diagram of a typical diagonal base cabinet installation with required fillers.*

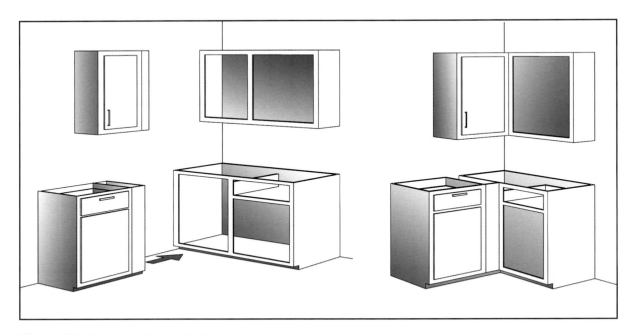

Figure 2.21 *Diagram of a typical blind corner base installation.*

Accommodating Adjacent Material Overhang Requirements

The countertop overhang extends beyond the side and the front of the base cabinet. Crown moulding extends beyond the side and the front of a cabinet. The relationship of countertop and moulding overhangs to the product they are installed on, as well as the walls they are set against, must be clearly detailed in the elevations. Do not forget to allow space around door and window casings for the cabinet end, countertop/backsplash overhang and moulding treatment. Clients must understand why slivers of wall space are often included in the kitchen design.

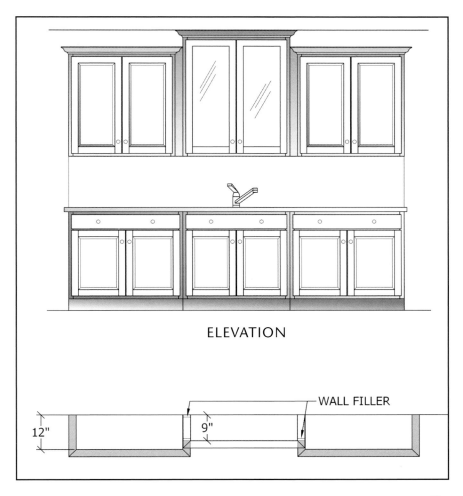

Figure 2.22 *Elevation of typical installation of base and wall cabinets with overhanging crown moulding and full backsplash.*

Figure 2.23 *Elevation of similar typical installation with 4-inch backsplash detail.*

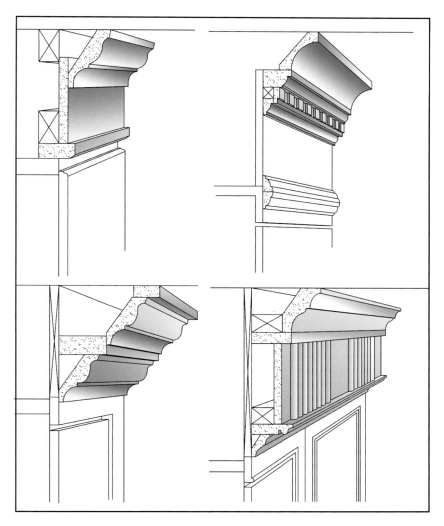

Figure 2.24 *Diagram of wall space required for stacked moulding installation.*

About Cabinet Door Movement

DOOR STABILITY: SWELLING AND SHRINKING

It is the norm in our industry that wood used to manufacture cabinets has a moisture content approximating that which will be present in the finished installation. This is important in a cabinet featuring a factory finish. It is critical when unfinished cabinetry is shipped to a jobsite.

Until the wood is finished, there is a greater chance for it to absorb moisture from the surrounding atmosphere at the jobsite. Because of this concern, it is often specified that unfinished cabinetry cannot be delivered to a jobsite and stored in an non-air-conditioned space. For example, shipping cabinets built in Salt Lake City, Utah, to Key West, Florida, and then storing them in an non-air-conditioned garage on the jobsite can spell disaster as the wood swells in the new environment. Managing the delivery and installation process means keeping a careful eye on the moisture content at the jobsite.

Regardless of how carefully this process is monitored, it should be expected that doors will grow or shrink during heating and cooling seasons in the home. Typically, this is most evident the first year the wood is installed. Less movement can be expected after the first year.

One of the biggest misconceptions a consumer has is that the cabinet doors will be absolutely straight, and that the margins between doors will be precisely the same dimension. Oftentimes, consumers assume a door is defective and must be replaced because of a misunderstanding about acceptable wood movement.

Our industry is not scientific. The consumer must understand that the overall size of the door and the wood specie selected affect how much that door will grow and shrink as it acclimates to the ambient moisture content in the air in the home.

One design firm includes the following information in their project specifications:

> *"Once installed, expect to see some shrinking during the first winter months, and some swelling during the first summer as the kitchen adjusts to its new setting. Swelling is to be expected in our inset cabinetry, which allows 3/32 inch allowance between the case and our hand-sanded doors. If cabinetry is exposed to excessive moisture, the wood will swell more. For example, a*

24-inch wide door with a 20-inch panel could swell as much a 1/8 inch—all this movement is taken up on the pull side because the hinge holds the door stable. Should some swelling occur, do not sand and refinish the door, because of the expected reversal of the swell during the warmer season."

Which directions will the door expand?

Framing will expand outward in all directions. This is the reason why paired doors or inset doors hit each other or get tight inside the front frame. It is also why full overlay doors are typically hung on the cabinet with a 1/8-inch gap between doors and cabinets.

Space between drawer fronts and drawers must also be considered in both frame and frameless cabinetry. The wider or higher the door front, the more chance of wood movement problems. Rarely are drawer fronts made from a solid wood slab because of these expansion issues.

How do five-piece doors expand?

When five-piece doors are used, the door is designed for the panel to expand. Normally, the panel is glued or pinned in the middle of the top and bottom rails allowing the panel to move (grow) in width for seasonal expansion. In addition, or alternatively, the door engineering may include spacers (positioned in the rabbit groove of the door frame). These spacers are flexible, allowing the "floating" panel to expand without opening the frame joints or shrink without causing a "rattle" sound because of a loose fitting center panel.

How do mitered doors expand?

Mitered doors usually have wider framing than stile-and-rail doors. They are typically designed to have a small opening in the inside corner. This opening will close first during expansion before putting pressure on the mitered joint.

Moisture Effect on Painted Doors

In cases with increased moisture, panel staves are affected. A combination of staves growing at different rates and a slight increase in the radial direction are highly visible in painted doors. Framing joints will also be more visible with increased moisture.

TIPS FROM THE MASTERS

How does wood knowledge impact your design?

- Some species expand more than others. Know the specs for the specie you have selected.

- The wider the framing, the more chance for expansion problems.

- Solid wood raised panels will expand more than plywood panels. Because of the monolithic nature of MDF panels, they will not show stave (solid wood strips laid up to form the center panel in a wood five-piece door) movement lines in paint.

- Do not recommend mitered doors and inset doors for high-risk areas.

- Show client examples/samples of movement lines in painted wood panels.

- Show examples of what is acceptable and what would be replaced.

What affects moisture in the house?

- Is the house located in a "high risk" area, such as near water?

- Is the house under construction? If yes, are the windows installed or open a lot of the time?

- Are they still putting up drywall or painting in the house? Grouting the tiled floor? Cementing garage or basement floors? These construction activities increase the moisture content in the air.

- Is the home climate controlled? Air conditioning? Dehumidification?

- Where are the components of the new kitchen being stored during construction? In the basement? Garage? Was there new cement poured on this site?

- Is there an indoor pool? A hot tub close by?

What you can do to minimize the risk of wood expansion?

- Educate the homeowners so that they understand a relative humidity level of at least 50% must be maintained all year round. That might require air conditioning in the summer and a humidifier in the winter.

- Deliver all cabinetry (especially moulding) to the jobsite at least three days before the installation begins. The wood parts can then acclimate to the environment, which will minimize moulding joints opening up after installation.

- If joints do open up during construction, insist on climate control prior to adjustments/replacements.

- Be prepared to remove doors/drawers and put in a climate-controlled area until site is controlled.

Question—when should a kitchen be installed?

Answers ...

- Windows and doors installed.

- Drywall is completed.

- Flooring is installed (and protected).

- Painting is completed.

- Cement work is mostly cured. This varies based on humidity levels, from geographic area to geographic area, and at different times of the year. Check with your general contractor.)

- Home is climate controlled.

DOOR WARPAGE

A Positive Bow: A convex curve in the door (when the wood member bulges away from the frame) is called a "positive bow."

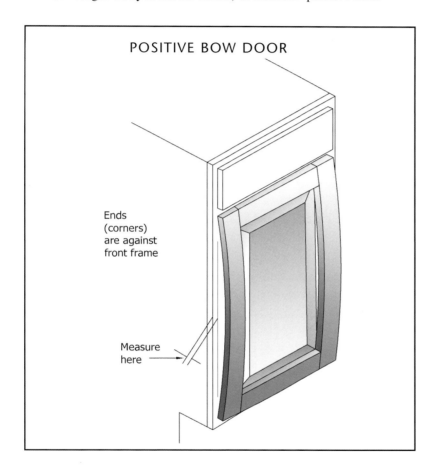

Figure 2.25 *A positive bow.* (Courtesy of Conestoga Wood Specialties Corporation)

A Negative Bow: When the cabinet door warps inwardly it is a concave curve, and called a "negative bow."

Figure 2.26 *A negative bow.*
(Courtesy of Conestoga Wood
Specialties Corporation)

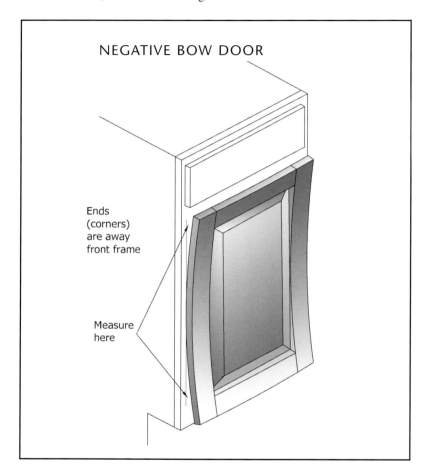

NEGATIVE BOW DOOR

Ends
(corners)
are away
front frame

Measure
here

TWISTED DOOR

Opposite Ends
(Corners are away
from front frame)

Figure 2.27 *A twisted door.*
(Courtesy of Conestoga Wood
Specialties Corporation)

Even with such attention to detail, wood is still a product of nature. While certain characteristics are unique to each species, a piece of veneer produced from an individual log will have its own characteristics. This is the true beauty of wood.

Color Variations

Expect color variation within a species. Many factors present during the life of the tree, including the soil types and minerals found in the soil, along with water levels, available sunlight and temperature influence wood color.

Genetic composition also plays its part in creating variety within a species. Hardwood trees originate from seeds, root sprouts and stump sprouts. Trees originating from seeds contain genetic variables from two parent trees, while sprouts from roots and stumps will be genetically identical to the parent tree. Because of these variables, trees of the same species from one area might be quite different from other areas.

Natural Wood Characteristics

- *Pin knot.* Knots vary in size, shape, structure and color.

- *Ray flecking.* Ray flecking is visible in hardwood species that are quarter-sawn and have rays. The rays are strips of cells that extend radially within a tree, and primarily store food and transports it horizontally. Red Oak and White Oak are most commonly noted for this characteristic.

- *Bird peck.* Woodpeckers produce a small hole, which is the starting point for a brown to blackish mineral streak. Bird peck is common in hickory and maple.

- *Worm tracks.* A worm track is a small, narrow, yellowish to brown streak, caused by Cambium Miners feeding beneath the bark from the branches to the roots. Tiny burrows are filled in by new fell growth and become imbedded in the wood as the tree continues to grow. Worm tracks, also called "pith flecks," are common in maple.

- *Gum spots.* Peach Bark Beetles and Cambium Miners are the main cause of gum spots. The feeding insects cause injury to the living portion of the bark, leading to the formation of gum spots in the wood as the tree continues to grow. Also known as "pitch pockets," gum spots are common in cherry.

- *Mineral streaks.* A darkened or discolored wood area caused by the minerals the tree extracts from the soil. A tree can be either mineral streaked or mineral stained. Mineral streaks appear as a blackish blue, well-defined line or area running parallel with the grain. Mineral streaks are commonly found in maple and birch and sometimes in oak and cherry. It is also known as spalting (a by-product of the rotting process that is carried out by a vast array of stain, mold and decay fungi that are found naturally on the forest floor), such as spalted maple.

- *Sapwood.* The sapwood of a tree conducts water up the tree stem and may contain some living cells. Sapwood can be lighter in color than hardwood. Sapwood is usually toward the outside of the tree as compared with the heartwood.

INSPECTING THE FINISH ON WOOD SURFACES

The Kitchen Cabinet Manufacturers' Association (KCMA) approved testing labs adhere to the following guideline for inspecting a finished wood surface:

> *"Lighting shall be from an overhead white fluorescent light with bulb(s) positioned parallel to the floor and having an intensity of 75 to 100 foot-candles (807 to 1076 lux) on the surface. View at an eye-to-specimen distance of approximately 30 – 36 inches (762 to 914.4 mm) and at an angle of approximately 45 degrees. Direct sunlight or other angle light sources, which will accentuate or minimize the effect, shall be avoided."*

THE PUNCHLIST: MANAGING THE LIST AND THE CLIENT

Even though designers carefully explain all these types of technicalities and variables of a project, many seasoned professionals agree that problem jobs can still grow out of good jobs. Common reasons are:

- Imprecise communication from project manager to subcontractor/contract installer.

- Indecisive/incomplete preparation of punchlists with owner or owner's agent collaboration.

- Problems occurring because of a disorganized jobsite, over scheduling with too many trades in the room at one time, and lack of respect for the client's existing property or the new materials being installed.

- A lack of urgency on everyone's part in completing punchlist items. The items on this list are, oftentimes, simple initially— but they grow out of proportion as the client begins losing confidence in you and your team because the project just does not seem to get finished.

Clearly, the path to any profitable project is 100% accuracy in the design details, product specifying, measuring and product ordering before the installation begins. In reality, once the installation starts, it may be quite evident that a 100% performance was not accomplished during the preparation for the project. Your commitment to excellence in communication, and your expectation of professionalism from every person on the jobsite will make the difference. Creating an organized approach to managing the punchlist is the best tool you can utilize to ensure the project is done on time, on budget, resulting in a happy client.

The Designer's Responsibility for Punchlist Development

It is the designer's responsibility to oversee the preparation of a list of items to be completed to the client's satisfaction. The list is called the punchlist. Here are some pointers from seasoned professionals.

- *Focus on precise communication with the consumer.* Maintain your business relationship with the consumer through the end of the project. (You can become best friends later.) Make sure the client understands some items on a punchlist at the end of the project are to be expected. A punchlist does not indicate poor workmanship. Additionally, make sure the clients understand that they have responsibilities in the preparation of the punchlist, as do you and your craftspeople.

- *Start the punchlist early.* Inspect the jobsite at several points, such as before the wall studding is closed in, just before the cabinets arrive, as soon as the cabinets are installed, and after the counters are in-place. Keep a copy of the punchlist in the job book.

- *Talk to the client.* There is nothing that will turn a good client sour faster than days that go by with no communication about the reordered parts or when the inspection will take place.

- *If possible, order replacement/repair/missing items as soon as they are detected.* Make sure you know where to ship these items if the location is different from where materials for a new job are accepted by your organization.

TIPS FROM THE MASTERS

- Prepare a list once and then work against it. Remember, "Write the list, then work against the list to get it done." The client signs each list to insure understanding and agreement.

- Start the punchlist in one specific corner of the room, and then move in a full circle around that space so that nothing is overlooked. When meeting with the client, always look for one item that you know needs to be replaced or repaired and point it out to the client so they are comfortable with you as the senior inspector on the project.

- If a client raises an objection that is not realistic (a pebble-size imperfection in a stucco wall surface, for example, or a worm tracking mark in a maple veneer), stop what you are doing and address the product quality level immediately. If necessary, use industry documentation to demonstrate the product, as delivered, is within industry standards.

- Travel with portable construction lights in your car because, oftentimes, designers are meeting with clients in the evening at their jobsite and there is no electricity—and no lighting—to the room under construction. With lighting, you can inspect the room carefully together.

- Keep in touch with your clients. Keep them informed as to what is going on in writing, by telephone or e-mail. Also, if any of the costs associated with items on the punchlist are really better categorized as change orders, provide a copy of the change order to the client. If there is going to be a disagreement—handle it now so there are no surprises when the final bill is presented.

- When working on large, luxurious projects always include a "punchlist contingency fund" dollar amount in your estimate, so if the client does not like one particular door on the job—you do not have to argue about the wood specification. You can smile, replace the door, make the client happy, and protect your profits.

- Have a special area in your warehouse for any items received for a project that is in progress. All too often, small boxes arriving with hardware or another roll of wallpaper, or a small under-cabinet light can get lost in a warehouse filled with large cabinet orders awaiting delivery. Have a special racking system by the front door of the warehouse that is divided into bins. Then clip a label on the bin identifying the job name and number. Inspect any replacement material before storing in the bins. Send an e-mail from the warehouse to the designer each time a replacement item arrives so both the warehouse staff and the designer in charge of the project can keep track of what has arrived. This makes it easier for the designer—who is responsible for all ordering—to double-check with a manufacturer/supplier if something misses its scheduled delivery time.

TIPS FROM THE MASTERS (continued)

- If there are quite a few items on the list, separate the punchlist into each area of the house, and for each source or manufacturer. You do not want the cabinet manufacturer to wade through your list of touch-up points for the plumber or the painter.

- Update all punchlists at the end of the week on every project; make this a Friday afternoon ritual to keep you on-point. Start checking with manufacturers, installers or subcontractors on Thursday to make sure you have the correct update material for the punchlist. This also makes it easier to schedule service work the following week.

- Have a clear policy around punchlists and the installers on your team: no punchlist/no specific information = no pay to the installer and no future jobs. Until a client signs off that the job is complete to their satisfaction, there should be no final payments made to installers.

At the conclusion of the project, evaluate the punchlist so you can improve your presentation skills and project management abilities.

1. *The consumer does not have a realistic expectation about product performance, wood specie specifications, etc.* It is your job to make sure the client knows what they are going to receive before the product arrives. If the client's expectations are unrealistic, discuss it frankly and to the point the minute an observation/complaint/question is raised. Use industry standards or other material to prove your case. For example:

   A. The client's misconception that a cabinet door is "warped."

   B. The client's misunderstanding about the randomness of a hand-applied glaze finish.

   C. The client's misunderstanding about the appearance of a ceiling crown moulding when it must be fit against an out-of-square/out-of-plumb ceiling.

2. *Products that arrive damaged—from the manufacturer or shipping company.* It is the jobsite installer, project manager or other individual assigned to the site (or the warehouse manager's responsibility) to totally inspect all product and note such defects immediately so they can be repaired or replaced. Projects under the control of the designer which are being installed outside of your normal business area can be problematic. For example, wise designers schedule a trip to a far-away jobsite by either themselves or their representative to receive and accept cabinetry delivery. Never leave this task to an individual on the jobsite who does not report directly to your firm who sold the cabinets.

3. *Items that were ordered incorrectly, overlooked or are incorrect because of some related change that was made.*

Key areas of concern here are:

A. Incorrectly ordering moulding. See Chapter 3 for a detailed list of how to make sure you order moulding correctly.

B. Decorative hardware never ordered when the cabinets were ordered.

C. Appliance selections changed after the cabinet order was placed, resulting in appliance panels arriving at the jobsite that do not fit the final selection.

D. Decorative brackets or other architectural accoutrements that are shown on the plan, but never ordered by the designer.

4. *Jobsite damage.* Everyone visiting or working on the jobsite needs to be aware of how delicate materials are, and how costly it is to repair/replace damaged product if a careless installer places a tool belt on a new counter or a ladder falls against a stainless steel appliance. Steps needed to minimize a punchlist include:

• A jobsite that is swept clean every night

• A staging set in the garage or adjacent living space that is managed by the design firm

• An installation team (whether a direct employee, subcontractor or contractor) who respect each others work

• A design firm adamant about providing proper dust barriers, drop cloths and other protective coverings

Dealing with Upset Clients

Regardless of how hard you try, sometimes a frustrated client will get angry with you. Successful designers have a strategy in-place to follow when clients are upset about the progress of a project, disappointed in an element of a project, or are just difficult people.

Identify what has upset the client (particularly valuable if the job did start well).

• Were all client design, product and installation expectations met?

• Could there have been a family disagreement or other unrelated household incident that sparked the unhappiness?

• *The manufacturer's rep is not carrying a checkbook.* Be aware that it is not uncommon for the client to assume that there is a discount, rebate, or free product to be had. As leverage, this type of client may begin the conversation by pointing out every conceivable imperfection, or, may ask for a resolution to be determined one issue at a time. Experienced pros just listen.

A good rep first records everything they observe, as well as all issues raised by the client. The rep never addresses issues under discussion one by one. This recommended "holistic" approach to gathering all issues troubling the consumer before any one item is reviewed allows all parties to establish a priority ranking of questions/concerns, as well as identify if there are a series of related problems. When everyone has agreed on the total list, the discussion can be structured to address like items together, or in a prioritized fashion.

TIPS FROM THE MASTERS

Money should never be the solution. If at all possible, a product replacement or repair is best. It is more beneficial to the manufacturer to have a satisfied client than it is to pay a client off to live with a cabinet they are not happy with.

CHAPTER 3: What Every Designer Should Know About Construction

The level of installation knowledge required on the designer's part varies according to the type of kitchen and bath projects the firm typically creates, the designer's project management responsibilities, and the type of structure being built or being remodeled. In prior chapters we have discussed business models in which the designer has extensive project management responsibility, as well as those where the individual has little. The different types of construction sites (where the installation process will occur) will be our focus in this chapter.

Jobsite Dynamics: New House vs. Old House

The jobsite dynamics for a new home under construction or an existing project being renovated are very different. Following are some of the key things that differentiate these two sites.

New Construction	Remodeling
Sometimes working with a homeowner	Always working with a homeowner
New materials and site	Working with existing conditions
Dirt and dust don't matter	Cleanliness matters
Client does not yet have emotional attachment to the home	Client is emotionally attached to the home
There may not be neighbors to worry about	Neighbors to worry about
No details to match	Many details to match
Very predictable schedule pattern	Unpredictable schedule pattern
Pets or children will not be living onsite	Pets and children onsite
Sometimes many homes under contract in one location	Usually project locations miles apart

Dwelling Dynamics: Detached Single-Family Dwelling vs. Multi-Family High-Rise Dwelling

The type of dwelling also significantly impacts the cost of installing projects, the project scheduling and site accessibility.

Detached Single-Family Dwelling	Multi-Family High-Rise Dwelling
Designer works with homeowner and contractor directly.	Working with commercial contractors, building superintendents or other's agent rather than owner directly.
Scheduling is determined between owner/ owner's agent and kitchen designer.	Restricted schedule for access for the apartment/condo. Noise is a big issue.
No elevators/delivery issues exist.	Elevator size, availability and protection requirements extensive.
No parking restrictions apply. Reasonable distance from the worker's truck/delivery truck location and the site.	Parking restrictions exist. Debris collection areas may be nonexistent or very limited.
Working hours are at the discretion of the designer and client, with normal courtesies extended to neighbors regarding early or late hours or weekend working.	Working hours may be limited.
	Protection of common areas will be required Before beginning work take digital images of the general public area leading to the area you will be working in, paying close attention to existing damage to door casings, floors, walls and stairwells to eliminate the uncertainty about the original damage at the completion of the job.

In the NKBA Design Survey Forms, a special checklist is included
to make sure you take note of various conditions.

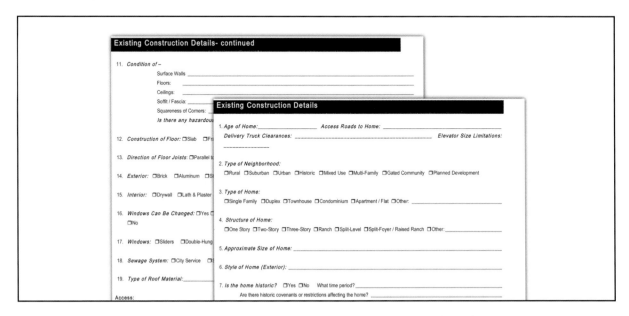

Figure 3.1 *The NKBA Kitchen and Bath Design Survey Forms.*

The Extra Cost of Working in an Inhabited Space

Regardless of whether it's a detached single-story home, a twin/duplex residence, or a high-rise condominium project, it costs more money to do work in a residence that is inhabited by the family.

Key site conditions impacting costs are as follows:

- A temporary kitchen needs to be set up.

- Space must be cleared onsite for storage.

- Onsite or street-side parking delays start time.

- Set-up and close-down of jobsite each day in a safe manner takes longer.

- Moving from the project exterior through finished and/or inhabited spaces to the work site takes longer.

- Removal of debris may require costly installation of trash container to house exterior, construction of special work entrance and exit to the work zone, modifications of interior door/wall areas to close off the renovated space.

- Setting up dust barriers takes more time.

- Exchanging pleasantries with the client at the site, keeping a watchful eye out for children or pets, visiting briefly with neighbors and friends who stop by to "take a look," working with building inspectors, and interfacing with the building superintendent take minutes—that add up to hours—not devoted to work.

- Setting up appropriate lighting for jobsite inspections with the client requires special mobile fixture equipment onsite.

- The requirement of a "clean" jobsite requires more careful cleaning in a renovation project than it does at a new construction site.

- Because the work zone is contained to the room being remodeled, adjacent spaces are, oftentimes, not available for storage, workbench, tool set-up, or the like. Therefore, traveling between the site and an exterior staging area takes more time.

TIPS FROM THE MASTERS

Removal of debris is even more costly in bathroom projects than in kitchens because a kitchen normally has an exit through a utility or mud room, into a garage, or to an acceptable staging area outside the dwelling.

Building Permits and Codes

Chapter 2 of the NKBA book *Kitchen & Bath Systems* is an excellent chapter covering U.S. and Canadian building codes, as well as those affecting mechanical and electrical systems. This chapter also has excellent guidelines for a designer to follow when scheduling jobsite inspections and/or working directly with the building department personnel onsite.

Building code information is also available in the NKBA books *Residential Construction, Kitchen Planning* and *Bath Planning*.

In addition there are several other tips from seasoned professionals in our industry that will help make the job go much smoother as you interface with the inspectors.

TIPS FROM THE MASTERS

- If you have a question about a code—call or visit the inspector's office to get clarification. Or, consult a contractor who has had experience with the code item—typically an inspector will not give advice due to liability concerns.

- Build the proper time for inspection and re-inspection into your schedule.

- Make sure it is clear who is responsible to wait at the jobsite for the inspector: you, one of the installers, or the owner or owner's agent. (If at all possible, a senior member of your team should be onsite to welcome the inspector and insure a clear understanding of any issues they raise.)

- Check your work carefully. It will benefit you to get a reputation for having your work ready and up to code. Inspectors "get to know" the better firms in their area—if they have no reason to believe you are going to try to "slip something past them," the inspector will work much closer with you.

- Get the inspector's name, if possible. Everyone likes to be addressed by their name—and inspectors are no different.

- Be sociable—small pleasantries may help you begin establishing an ongoing rapport with this professional. Be nice!

- If the inspector "flags" (turns down) any part of the project, make sure you understand exactly what the violation is and what you need to do to correct it. The designer may be in a situation where the inspector is wrong or there is vagueness to the code—be proactive and go to the appropriate department to get clarification.

- Ask questions about future potential problems: are there any areas of work coming up that you are not sure of? Take the time to ask about them while the inspector is on the job. You will be able to find out exactly what the inspector will be looking for when they return to the job.

TIPS FROM THE MASTERS

- Pay particular attention to the information in *Kitchen & Bath Systems* as it relates to the relationship between the interior canopy size of the hood and the distance from the cooking surface to the bottom of the hood. The system will not work if the hood is too small!

- Whenever you are planning to install a commercial sized range hood that finishes at the edge of the range top or stove—consider the client's height: the bottom edge of the hood is just above the primary user's eye level. This can be very dangerous.

- Realize that determining the vent path is an important part of your conceptual planning. Use the NKBA Survey Form to detail the construction constraints in a renovation project. If ductwork is through the basement, or down to the basement and out to an exterior wall, how long will the run be? If you are moving the ventilation system, what path will the vent ductwork follow?

- When thinking about the duct path study the checklist on Page 60 of *Kitchen & Bath Systems*—realize the limits on the number of elbows that you can plan and the distance from elbow to elbow. Learn about duct sizing as well. If the preferred duct path is longer than efficiency standards, consider adding an in-line secondary fan. Discuss such a solution with the manufacturer's customer service staff and your HVAC contractor. Do not vary from manufacturer specifications! If required by the owner, get a signed waiver before you proceed.

- Explain to your client that it is a good habit to turn the ventilation blower on "low" when starting to cook—this generates air currents within the room that aid in ventilation while keeping noise to a minimum.

- Make sure you understand the requirement for "make-up" air in a kitchen system, including a hood with a 300+ cfm.

- Make sure your client appreciates the "healthy living" benefit of a well-ventilated bathroom. Fungus and mildew growth can be inhibited or eliminated if moist air is continually removed from the room.

The Plumbing System

Modifying/adding to or replacing the plumbing system in a renovation project takes a solid base of knowledge on the designer's part. *Kitchen & Bath Systems* discusses this system in detail in Chapter 6 (The Hot and Cold Water Supply) and Chapter 7 (Drain, Waste and Vent Systems). Chapter 8 also gives the designer a basic overview of plumbing fixtures, appliances and accessories. More detailed information is included in the NKBA book, *Kitchen & Bath Products* where the details of multiple showers and specialty fixtures sometimes specified for master suites are covered.

TIPS FROM THE MASTERS

- Read the information in *Kitchen & Bath Systems* carefully! It will tell you the different ways you can vent a sink placed in an island. Verify local codes first: you may need to include a decorative post at the edge of the island to conceal necessary ductwork.

- Try not to move a toilet. Because the toilet must be vented, and it is one of the fixtures (along with garbage disposals) that carries solid waste in a drainage system based on gravity, it is the most difficult plumbing fixture to relocate. If your design proposal is based on relocating the toilet, have the plumbing contractor inspect the site before you present the solution to the client.

- Do not try to replace a tub with a shower unless you have talked to the plumber about the drain size upgrades needed. A shower—with multiple heads—needs a bigger drain pipe than a standard tub. Moving the shower drain off center may make the area much more comfortable for standing.

- If you are using any of the new vessel bowls or vanity faucets that come out of the wall (rather than up through the vanity countertop), make sure the plumber knows this. You need to detail the exact, and we emphasize exact, location for the vanity faucet valves and spout water line rough-in location.

- If you have a tub with a series of controls, lay out the order you want these tub filler elements located. Think about the bather reclining in the tub: should both the hot and cold valves be on one side, or placed on opposite sides of the tub filler? Where do you want a hand-held shower installed?

- When planning an elaborate master bath make sure the client understands the hot water needs for their new fixtures. Typically, a water heater serving only the new bath will be required. If the hot water supply is a long distance from the bath, a circulation pump should also be specified. Lastly, large bathtubs will take a long time to fill unless a larger supply line and a high-volume fill valve are planned and installed.

- Do not overlook the access panels required for the jetted tub motor or the steam shower system.

- Learn all the details of a steam shower before suggesting one. For example, the location and drain for the generator needs to be plotted on the plan. A 240-amp circuit must be available at the service box. The proper ergonomic seat size and a within-reach system control panel are part of the plan.

- There are so many new products offered for the spa bath. Make sure you know the details of these items before suggesting them. For example, understand the difference between a jetted tub and an air bubbler system.

- Be very careful when specifying the rough-in plumbing center line for 30-inch to 42-inch wide "combo" vanity cabinets. These cabinets center the lavatory in the cabinet countertop, but require an off-center plumbing rough-in location to accommodate the one operable drawer in the cabinet.

- If you are suggesting a free-standing pedestal lavatory in a bath, or a special furniture-type vanity, make sure the plumber has the spec sheets so they can locate the area.

Framing Systems

Understanding framing systems is also important. Study the diagrams on pages 82, 83 and 84 in *Residential Construction*.

TIPS FROM THE MASTERS

- In typical residential construction, all door or window openings in exterior load bearing walls have a header above them. Therefore, you cannot run windows or doors all the way to the ceiling.

- When changing an opening in a wall, plan on completely refinishing the entire wall on both sides, and specify how the flooring in the new opening will be finished.

- When considering installing a pocket door on a renovation project, make sure you verify there are no plumbing pipes or HVAC duct work in the wall space that will be occupied by the pocket door. Realize the pocket portion of the opening requires a header as well. Do not plan any bathroom accessory or electric outlet installation in the wall area occupied by the pocket.

- When removing a wall, know how to determine if it is a load bearing wall or a non-load bearing wall. Study carefully the information in *Residential Construction* regarding interior walls and ceilings to better understand the role a partition serves, as well as what sort of specialized framing is required for tub platforms, shower enclosures, arched doorways and suspended ceilings. Excellent information is included about modifying existing walls and ceilings.

- Make sure you are familiar with building codes so you know when you must retain an engineer to design and "sign off" on structural changes you are proposing to the client.

- Measure passageways, hallways and doors to insure materials can be delivered to an interior room being remodeled. For example, an oversized tub or a one-piece shower may not fit up the stairs, down the hall and through the doorway to a second floor master bathroom suite.

- When planning a project in a multi-story building, verify the framing system used and the wall structure. Building systems were very different 100 years ago. For example, high-rise buildings often have steel—not wood—studs. Solid brick walls may be behind the plaster on a common wall in an urban townhouse.

INTERIOR SURFACES

Interior surfaces—both the substrate and finished materials—are also an important part of the plan and the budgeting. In *Residential Construction,* interior surfaces from the past such as plaster, as well as gypsum board (drywall) and the cementous boards today are covered in Chapter 12.

TIPS FROM THE MASTERS

- Make sure the painting contractor properly masks and covers installed cabinetry and countertops to avoid splatter on new surfaces.

- Realize that even a small patch in an existing textured wall will require a full-wall (corner-to-corner) texture coating to provide a consistent surface appearance.

- In a renovation project, have the plaster experts inspect a room with cracking or sagging plaster. Extensive rework to stabilize the old plaster may be required before the new skim coat or plaster mix can be applied.

- Know your local codes regarding waterproof wall materials acceptable for use behind wet walls in bathroom tub/shower areas.

Counter Surface/Backsplash Surfaces

Each material you specify has its own inherent set of planning concerns that, if ignored, can cause problems at the jobsite.

A major area of planning should be the countertops installed in projects. The International Solid Surface Fabricators Association (ISSFA, www.issfa.org) conducts training programs for their installation specialists—known as "field technicians." This organization echoes the position NKBA places on proper installation management in its programming. Considering counter surfacing, ISSFA breaks the installation into 16 separate, identifiable, simple steps. Looking at these steps, once again, we see that the field technician and the project manager are interdependent on one another. The project will not be successful without the full cooperation and successful execution of each area of responsibility.

If either one does not meet these set of standards, the other entity will fail. As you look at the following list, note that only 11 of the steps directly relate to the field technician. The other 5 are management responsibilities.

ORDERING MOULDING

Figure 3.2 *When something is missed – this is what can happen!*
(Courtesy of David Newton, CMKBD)

One of the most common mistakes made when ordering cabinets and decorative mouldings is miscalculating the quantity of moulding lengths needed to complete the project. When cabinet parts are missed on the order, ordered incorrectly or not ordered in sufficient quantity, a great deal of time and money is wasted during the reorder process.

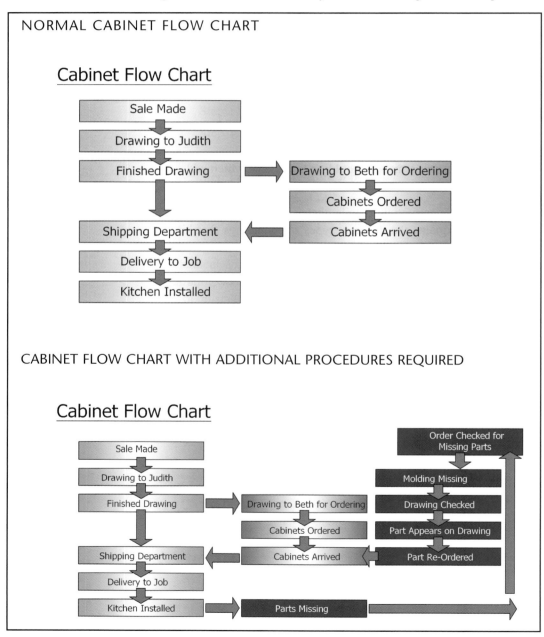

Joseph Matta, CKD, of Masterworks Kitchens, Goshen, N.Y., shares his years of experience around the best way to lay out a moulding plan for a kitchen or bath, and calculate the proper lengths of mouldings.

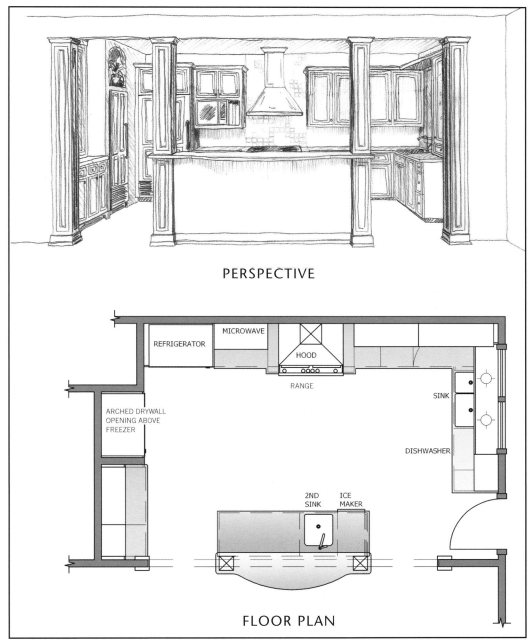

Figure 3.3 *Ordering moulding.* (Courtesy of Ellen Cheever, CMKBD, ASID and Jeffrey Holloway, CKD.)

Step No. 1

- Identify the projection of moulding and lengths of moulding available.

- Determine usable length of moulding based on manufacturer's specifications.

- Select one corner to begin the moulding length calculation.

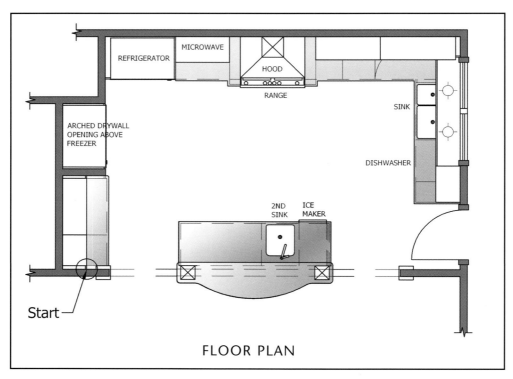

Figure 3.4 *Ordering moulding: Step No. 1.*

Step No. 2

Add the lengths needed, rounding up to the next full foot.

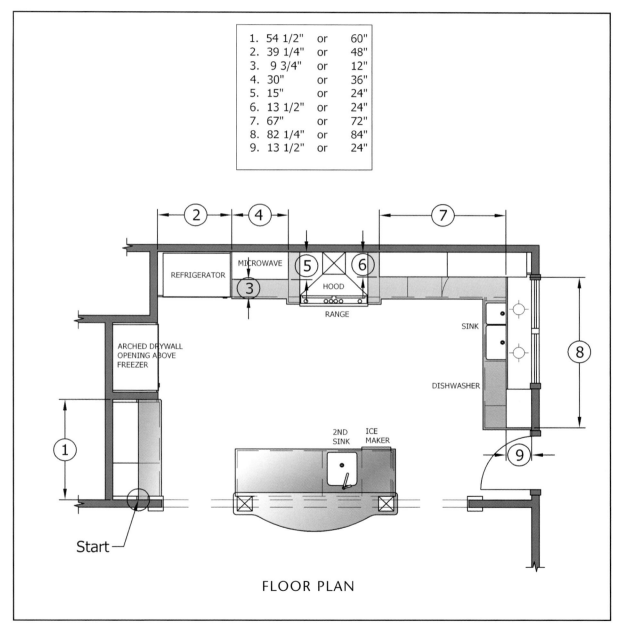

1.	54 1/2"	or	60"
2.	39 1/4"	or	48"
3.	9 3/4"	or	12"
4.	30"	or	36"
5.	15"	or	24"
6.	13 1/2"	or	24"
7.	67"	or	72"
8.	82 1/4"	or	84"
9.	13 1/2"	or	24"

FLOOR PLAN

Figure 3.5 *Ordering moulding: Step No. 2.*

Step No. 3:

Start with the longest length required, add the various lengths to determine the total number of pieces required from the proceeding step.

Step No. 4:

Consider the wood selection.

- Are there any moulding splice joints? If so, add one length.

- Does the wood specie graining require some wood sorting? If so, add at least one additional length.

- Does the wood's finish vary to the point some selection will be necessary at mitered corner joints? If so, add a length.

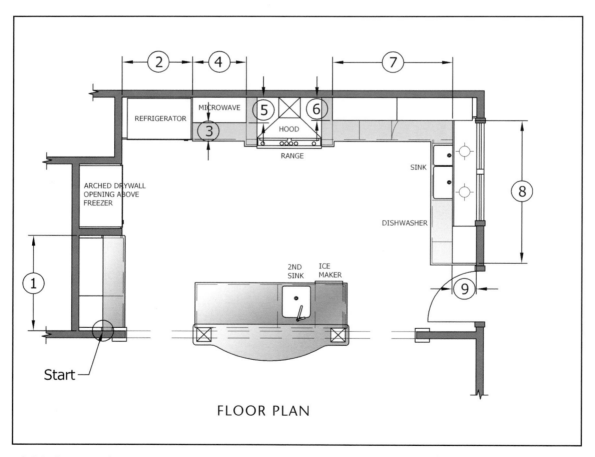

Figure 3.6 *Ordering moulding: Step Nos. 3 and 4.*

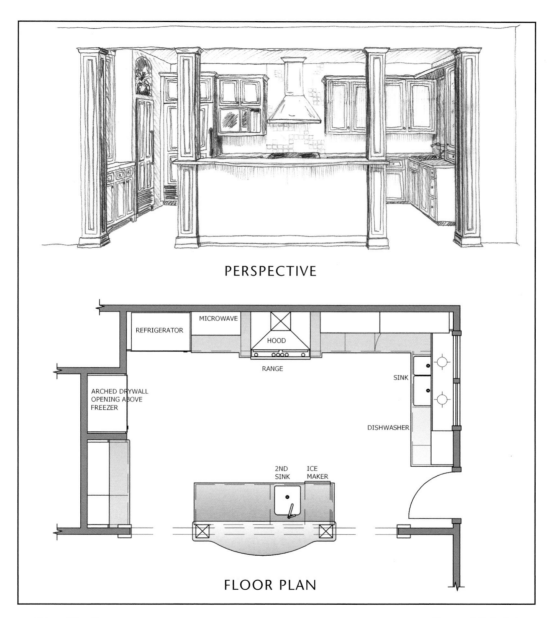

PERSPECTIVE

FLOOR PLAN

(Floor plan labels: REFRIGERATOR, MICROWAVE, HOOD, RANGE, SINK, DISHWASHER, ARCHED DRYWALL OPENING ABOVE FREEZER, 2ND SINK, ICE MAKER)

Step No. 5:

Allow for jobsite mistakes. Add an extra length.

Step No. 6:

Explain to the client that you will allow for extra moulding cuts, miters, damaged ends or questionable grain/color continuity. Decide whether you are going to leave this moulding on the job or return it to your stock.

Figure 3.7 *Ordering moulding: Step Nos. 5 and 6.*

HOW TO INSTALL
KITCHEN CABINETS

The cabinet installation begins at the jobsite weeks or even months before the cabinets arrive and the dimensions are double-checked. The installation continues when someone inspects the jobsite again before installing the drywall. At this point, verify that the mechanicals, HVAC and framing are as per plan. This step is critical on new construction projects to make sure workers follow the plan exactly. Measurement verification is necessary at this stage of new construction because it is common for windows to be 3 inches off or a wall to be perhaps as much as 4 1/2 inches out of place. To avoid headaches when the cabinets arrive, re-measure the entire site and verify that the cabinets will fit as planned, before closing in the room.

The installation draws closer with the delivery of the cabinets to the design firm's warehouse and/or the jobsite and a careful "transfer of title" takes place. Ideally, numbers on the outside of the packages coincide with numbers on the elevation and/or floor plan. The truck driver and the installation manager responsible for the project check the cabinets off as they arrive, inspecting each for damage and verifying the received items against an order acknowledgement and/or packing list.

The installation continues as the cabinets (either boxed, shrink wrapped or blanket wrapped) enter storage in a climate-controlled, safe area on the jobsite, protected from any damage that may occur as work progresses onsite.

The installation process continues when the installer arrives onsite and begins putting the cabinets in place.

Step No. 1:

Review the floor plan at the jobsite, marking each cabinet off on the wall and/or the floor to verify once again, that the mechanicals, HVAC and framing are as per plan. This is a good time to stand back and evaluate your plan details one more time. For example, do you need to shift a filler for better balance, or modify a roll-out shelf to accommodate the sink waste line rough-in? If there is a large, complicated island in the space, creating a template of the island in addition to verifying the mechanical rough-ins stubbed out of the floor is a good idea. Seasoned installation experts consider this cabinet check and layout review a critical part of a successful installation. Lastly, establish the cabinet delivery route through the house, checking doorway widths and any tight corner turning radius.

Figure 3.8 *Step No. 1:* Lay the floor
plan out on the floor and walls of the
jobsite.

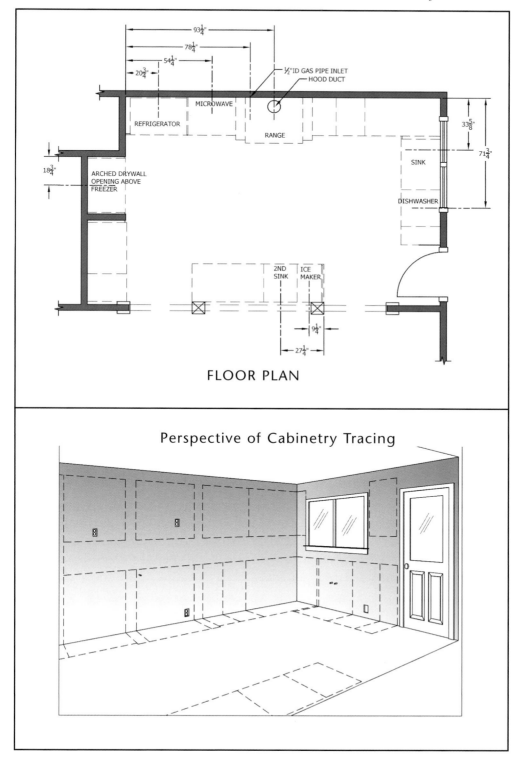

FLOOR PLAN

Perspective of Cabinetry Tracing

Step No. 2:

Secure the work area. Earlier information in Chapter 2 has identified the importance of protecting the work zone from the balance of the home.

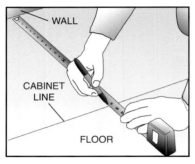

Figure 3.9 *Step No. 2:* Check the plans to make sure the correct cabinets have been delivered, and secure the room from the balance of the home.

Figure 3.10 *Step No. 3:* Check the floor level by measuring 18 inches from the wall for vanity cabinets and 21 inches for kitchen cabinets.

Step No. 3:

Identify any out-of-plumb or out-of-level surfaces the cabinets will be installed against or upon.

Check the floor level by measuring out 18 inches from the wall for vanity cabinets and 21 inches for normal kitchen cabinets. Use a straight edge and/or a long level to determine the high point in the floor. Many projects will have the high point of the room in a corner, as this is typically the place least likely to have settled. If this is the case, there may be so much drop at the front edge of the cabinets that the installer must scribe the back bottom edge of the base cabinets or shim up the front edge to meet the highest spot in the room. Be aware that some cabinets with toekicks that are edge banded with flake board may hold up better if they are not cut for scribing.

On some projects, where the finished floor is installed before the cabinets, it must be completely protected before this work begins. If there is no finished flooring installed, double-check the overall thickness of the substrate as well as the finished floor. You may need

Figure 3.11 *Step No. 3:* Determine the high point of the floor. Plan on shimming the cabinets up or scribing the cabinets down to accommodate the floor high point.

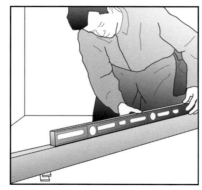

a built-up substrate if all of the cabinets must be shimmed up so that the finished floor can continue into a recess for an under-counter appliance. This step is critical so that the appliance is not locked in, and impossible to remove for servicing and/or replacing.

Step No. 4:

Transfer the high floor level mark to the wall and snap a plumb line at 34 1/2 inches off the finished floor. Or set the laser to 34 1/2 inches off the floor to determine the high and low spots. This tells the installer at what height the cabinets will actually be installed to insure they are level at the normal countertop finished height of 36 inches.

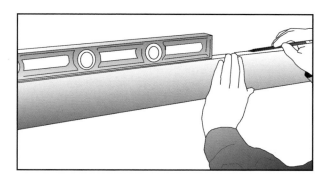

Figure 3.12 *Step No. 4:* Transfer the high level mark to the wall and snap a plumb line at 34 1/2 inches off the finished floor or set the laser to 34 1/2 inches off the floor to determine the high and low spots.

Step No. 5:

Base or mid-high cabinet heights other than a standard 34 1/2 inches are also marked: for example, a raised dishwasher installed at a 54-inch height, a mid-height oven cabinet installed at 60 inches.

Step No. 6:

Repeat the same "find the highpoint" exercise at the ceiling— finding the lowest spot on the ceiling wherever installing tall cabinets. This is of critical importance if cabinets will be installed to the ceiling. In the worst case scenario, an out-of-plumb sub floor with a dramatic high point combined in a room with an out-of-level ceiling and a low point spells disaster if 96-inch high units are trying to squeeze into a room with 96-inch high ceilings. Reduce the toekick on the tall units to accommodate such an out-of-square room.

Step No. 7:

Based on the backsplash dimensions (it may vary from 60 inches above the finished 36-inch high standard countertop to 24 inches above that dimension), mark another cabinet level for the wall cabinets.

Step No. 8:

Use a straight edge to determine the high and low spots along the back wall surface. This dimensioning will direct where you will need shims behind cabinets to provide a flush face in addition to a level surface.

Step No. 9:

If cabinets fit between walls or turn a corner, check the corners with a framing square so that you can adjust cabinets and countertops with a scribe that compensates for a tight wall, or finish with a filler to accommodate an out-of-square corner. Typically, the misalignment will be confined to the corner area, and the wall will not continue to run out-of-square its entire length. Be aware that the drywall compound used to finish the corner joint can cause a false read on a corner. Sometimes, more accurate dimensions can be found near the floor where the drywall compound is not present. It may also be necessary to set up a 3-4-5 triangle to test a larger area for square and get away from the corner for a better fit.

Here is how you use the mathematical equation to determine the squareness of a corner and, if out-of-square, how to determine if the corner is less than 90 degrees or more than 90 degrees.

- Starting in the corner, measure out of the corner along one wall to a dimension of 36 inches. Mark the wall with pencil.

- Return to the corner and measure out of the corner 48 inches along the second wall. Place a mark at this point.

- Measure the distance between these two marks. If the corner is square, the dimension between the two pencil marks will be 60 inches. If the dimension is less than 60 inches, the corner angle is less than 90 degrees and fillers will need to be cut down in width. If the dimension is more than 60 inches, the corner angle is more than 90 degrees and fillers may need to be added or cabinet widths increased.

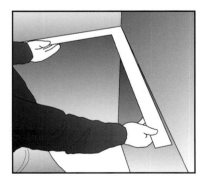

Figure 3.13 *Step No. 9:* Determine the squareness of any corners that cabinets will be placed against.

Step No. 10:

Locate the wall studs. The floor supports base cabinets if they have attached toekicks, or if they sit on a prefabricated sub-base. Fasten the wall cabinets directly to the studs, or use a hanging strip that is first attached to the walls, with the wall cabinet then cantilevering off this strip. See Step No. 18 for an option to consider when installing against a finished wall.

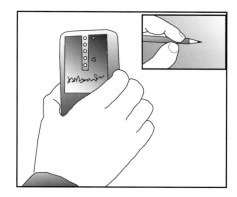

Figure 3.14A *Step No. 10:* Using an electronic stud finder makes the process easier and more accurate.

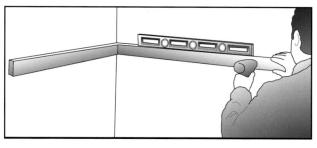

Figure 3.14B *Step No. 10:* You can attach a hanging strip before securing the cabinets.

TIPS FROM THE MASTERS

Industry experts vary in their recommendations regarding what to install first: the base cabinets or the wall cabinets. Talk to your installation experts to ascertain their preference. The key to a satisfied client is protecting each cabinet after installation. This outline continues with the assumption that you will install the base cabinets first.

Step No. 11:

Provide support for countertops for special cabinet considerations. Corner Lazy Susan base cabinets normally have a clipped back corner, allowing them to be moved through normal interior door widths. Therefore, the back wall will need to be "cleated" so that the countertop is supported. This may also be required behind an opening for a cooktop/range top, behind the wall for a dishwasher or other appliance. This becomes of critical importance if oversized or unusually heavy countertop materials are being used. Special partial walls or other supports may be required for countertop overhangs, open shelf systems or extended valance panels.

Step No. 12:

Move the cabinets into the room and position. Start in a corner. Remove skids from under toekicks. Remove doors and drawers and protect. Most installation specialists believe the one exception to this rule is for inset cabinet doors: the doors remain on the cabinet so that the installer can verify the door alignment during the installation process. If doors remain on the cabinet, take extra time to protect them from damage. Cover them, particularly if they are cherry wood and there is any direct sunlight close by.

Framed and frameless cabinetries are similar, yet each has unique features. The process of installing framed cabinetry is a little more forgiving than for a frameless cabinet. Install both plumb and level. Frameless units are more likely to rack if not shimmed and properly braced to avoid the twisting action caused by the tightening of screws where voids occur. Install the doors on the cabinets just before the final tightening of screws in the hanging strips. This will immediately reveal any racking, so you can correct the situation before it becomes severe.

Figure 3.15 *Step No. 12:* Move the cabinets into the room and position, starting in a corner. Remove doors and drawers and protect.

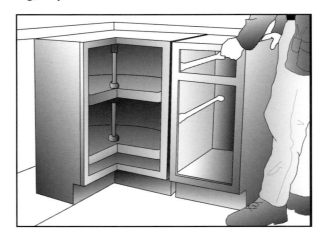

Step No. 13:

For typical cabinets with a sub-base (called a toekick) align and shim a corner cabinet as necessary to insure it is plumb. For decorative cabinets with furniture feet or columns/cabinet stiles extending to the floor, the original design should provide some means to modify the height. For example, decorative feet may incorporate a square scribing portion on the underside of the foot. It is cut to fit an unleveled floor, or is removed completely if a level floor surface exists. Or, decorative moulding can cover space resulting from an uneven floor between the floor and a shimmed column. If no such design adjustment exists, then hold a jobsite conference to decide how to lower the cabinet without compromising the height required for adjacent appliances.

Use some type of clamping device to hold adjacent cabinets together while installing the proper screws.

A master installer uses proper screws and the proper tools to install cabinets, with the necessary force (just enough, but not too much) to avoid splitting the face frame. The master installer then pulls adjoining cabinets together with screws. To do this:

- Drill starter hole approximately 6 inches from the top and bottom of face frame.

- Insert and tighten screw.

- After hanging, joining, aligning and shimming all base and wall cabinets, tighten screws in the hanging strips.

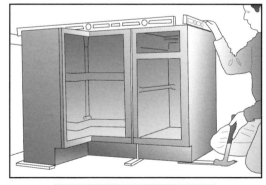

Figure 3.16A *Step No. 13:* Align and shim a corner cabinet to insure it is plumb.

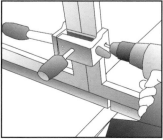

Figure 3.16B *Step No. 13:* Use a clamping device to hold adjacent cabinets together.

Step No. 14:

When shims are required at the back wall, place them directly over a stud. Then drill a pilot hole and screw the shim to the wall. Never use nails to fasten cabinets together or to secure cabinets to walls.

Figure 3.17 *Step No. 14:* Drill a pilot hole and screw the shim to the wall. Never use nails to fasten cabinets together or to secure cabinets to walls.

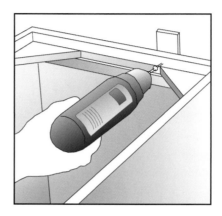

Step No. 15:

Cabinets that finish against a wall, against another cabinet that is deeper than the unit or meet one another in corners, will require extended stiles or scribes (often called fillers). A scribing or filler strip allows the installer to attach an extra strip of cabinet finish material to the case and then fit it against an out-of-plumb wall. The filler is normally set flush with the case, with a decorative panel placed on the front of the filler. This decorative panel will include a detailed edge echoing the finish on the door in custom cabinet work. In stock cabinet work, the filler normally blends with the door finish, but is a piece of plain wood or cabinet material set flush with the case. Alternatively, the filler can be an L-shaped or U-shaped element that has no detail but that can be set flush with the door.

Figure 3.18A and 3.18B *Step No. 15:* A scribing, filler strip or extended stile allows the installer to finish the cabinet elevation against a wall.

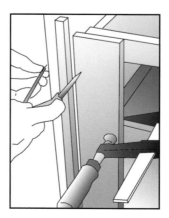
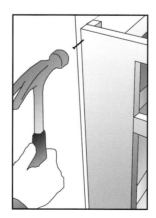

To scribe a filler, start by setting a marking compass to the width of the gap, and then place a strip of 1/2-inch wide masking tape along the filler board in the area where it needs to be trimmed. Clamp the board to the end face frame of the cabinet and trace the wall contour with the compass. Remove the board and cut along the scribed line with a jigsaw. The scribe will now mirror the wall dimension.

Step No. 16:

Now, cover the base cabinets for safety. This is a must because one of the worst offenders of scratches and indentations on base units is the installer's belt buckle or tape measure as the installer leans over the base units. BE AWARE! Install temporary plywood countertops or recycle the cardboard the cabinets came in to protect the cabinetry and provide a place for the installers to set their tools, as they install the wall cabinets.

TIPS FROM THE MASTERS

Trim the filler with a bevel cut, tapered away from the wall by several degrees and add a 1/32 of an inch to the width of the filler. This allows the sharp edge of the filler to imbed into the drywall and take away any slight imperfections in the cut or wall.

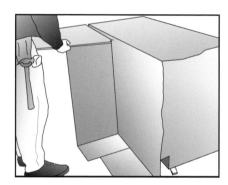

Figure 3.19 *Step No. 16:* Use plywood or the cardboard containers to protect the base cabinets.

Step No. 17:

Now, the installation moves to the tall and wall cabinets. If the design includes tall cabinets and the tops are to be at the same height as wall cabinets, install the "talls" just after the base units. They will then determine the precise height of the wall units.

A team of two installers is most efficient, but individual installers can work by bracing the wall or by using special tools designed to temporarily hold a wall cabinet in place while the lone specialist secures the unit to the wall. Sometimes a hanging strip supports the wall cabinets. If the cabinets are to be installed against a finished wall, such a plan will compromise the wall finish. A better alternative is to cut 1 inch x 2 inch strips 19 1/2 inches (for an 18 inch splash height), tapping them into the wall at the countertop height. The cabinets can then rest on these strips, or legs, until they are adjusted and screwed into place.

Normal base cabinets finish at 34 1/2 inches tall and are then topped by a 1 1/2 inch thick countertop making the finished base cabinet 36 inches off the finished floor. Backsplash height dimensions range from 15 – 18 inches high within U.S. cabinet manufacturing standards. International cabinet standards often call for a 16- to 24-inch backsplash area. Therefore, there is no industry standard. The elevation plans must clearly note what the backsplash dimension is from the top of the finished countertop to the bottom edge of the wall cabinet. It is important to have good elevations with accurate measurements and details so the installer knows what the designer is thinking.

While splash heights vary, determine the distance from any cooking surface to the underside of the ventilation hood by local codes and the appliance manufacturer's specifications. Do not specify this height or agree to any jobsite change recommendations without first verifying distances dictated by the building authorities or the manufacturer.

Figure 3.20 *Step No. 17:* Install a hanging strip to support wall cabinets during the installation.

Step No. 18:

Much like base cabinet installation, wall cabinet installation starts
in a corner. Wall cabinet corners may have a diagonal front, which
requires fillers on either side to insure the diagonal door can swing
clear of adjacent units. Alternatively, a square corner cabinet
occupying 24 inches of wall space in each direction (called a pie cut
cabinet) may be used. Thirdly, a blind corner cabinet may be installed
on one wall, extending into the corner, with a second wall cabinet
(separated by a scribe to insure handle clearance) fitting against this
cabinet at a 90-degree return. When installing a blind corner cabinet,
note that some manufacturers leave the blind portion open so it
appears to omit a small door. Closing this blind area off with light
grade plywood or a panel will keep the owner's items from falling into
the void left after installing the adjoining cabinet. The last typical
option is to install two wall cabinets at right angles to one another
(separated by fillers and/or scribes) or finished against a boxed-in
corner arrangement.

Figure 3.21 *Step No. 18:* Much like a
base cabinet installation, wall cabinet
installation also starts in a corner.

Step No. 19:

Before lifting any upper cabinets into place, the installation specialist normally pre-drills screw holes through the top and bottom hanging rails of the cabinet. Following the cabinet layout and the stud location marks on the walls, transfer the measurements to the cabinet back and drill pilot holes. When used properly, this system insures the installer will hit studs when driving the mounting screws through the finished back of the cabinet, passing through the hanging rail and the drywall to the stud behind.

Figure 3.22 *Step No. 19:* Proper planning will insure cabinet backs are drilled correctly to hit the wall studs.

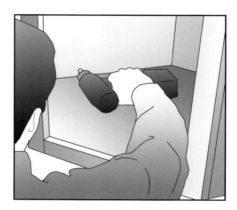

Step No. 20:

The sequence for installing wall cabinets resembles the sequence used for base cabinets. Some installers will assemble groups of upper cabinets as a single unit; other specialists prefer to hang each unit individually. A bar clamp is used to hold adjacent cabinets together and fasten loosely, the face frames remain aligned, flat, level and plumb. Such alignment is critical; any twist in the cabinet box or case will affect the fit of the doors.

Figure 3.23 *Step No. 20:* Use a bar clamp to hold adjacent cabinets together so the face frames remain aligned, flat, level and plumb.

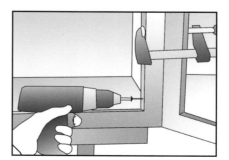

Step No. 21:

When the last upper cabinet is secure, install all soffit or moulding treatments. Then reinstall the shelves, interior accessories and doors on the cabinets. Next, drill for the decorative hardware if the manufacturing facility did not. While it is easier to layout hardware on the back of the door, drilling from the back may cause a "blowout" as the drill bit exits the face side of the cabinet. Clamp or hold a block on the face side of the door/drawer to reduce the likelihood of this happening, or drill from the front of the panel.

The elevation plans must clearly call out the exact location of the hardware. For example, a pull-out wastepaper basket cabinet will probably have the pull located in the center of the door, while other doors will have the pull opposite the hinge side. In many kitchens, drawers and doors feature different hardware. For some cabinet styles, the width of the stiles and rails determines where to place hardware. Any mistakes are costly and necessitate replacing full drawers and/or doors.

TIPS FROM THE MASTERS

Never leave the jobsite with doors out of alignment. If the doors are put back on the cabinets, adjust them before you leave. Otherwise, undoubtedly, a call will come from the client complaining the cabinets and doors are crooked.

Step No. 22:

Once the installer completes the cabinet set they methodically move around the room to adjust all door hinges and all drawer hardware to align the doors and drawers. At this time, putty any holes and/or finish touch-ups. Vacuum all cabinets—inside and out—and wipe with a damp tack cloth before the client inspects them.

Figure 3.24 *Step No. 22:* After the cabinet set is complete, adjust all the door hinges and drawer hardware.

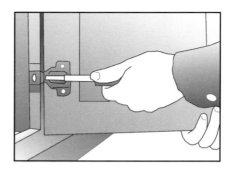

Figure 3.25 *Step No. 22:* Make sure all the doors are aligned properly.

Step No. 23:

Sweep the entire jobsite clean and dispose of all trash daily. Keep protective coverings on the cabinetry. Remember—the client waited weeks, if not months, for the cabinets to arrive and made substantial payments on the project to-date. The clients' first impression about the fit and finish of the cabinets can make a dramatic difference in how they perceive the overall quality of the job.

CUSTOM DESIGNED FEATURES

Often, designers will rough sketch, conceptualize or design a custom feature for a kitchen. But you can not estimate, manufacture or install such an idea until you first engineer the concept. The following examples are of the type of detailed engineering required to create a custom hood.

Figure 3.26 *Custom Hood.* The design by the kitchen specialist features a plaster bonnet top hood that extends beyond the adjacent wall cabinets. This hood features an elaborate plaster apron and plaster brackets that finish against a stepped bracket support held off the countertop to meet kitchen planning guidelines.

115

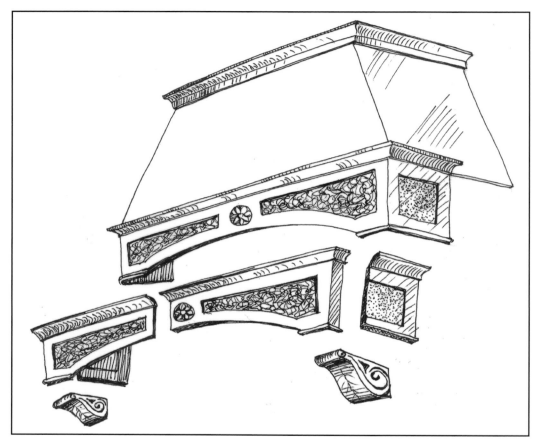

Figure 3.27 *The individual elements
of the architectural accoutrement.*
The first important element to determine
is the exact sizing and connecting
method that will be used in the out-
sourced plaster architectural element.

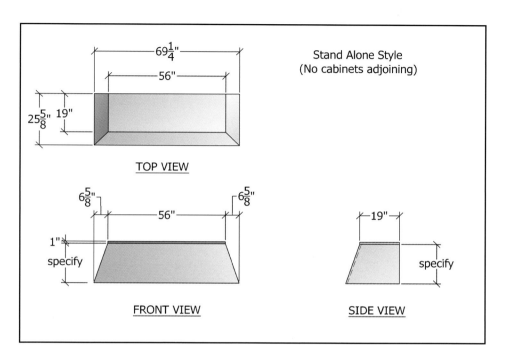

Stand Alone Style
(No cabinets adjoining)

TOP VIEW

FRONT VIEW

SIDE VIEW

Figure 3.28 *The overall size of the major elements.*

The second determination is the shape and configuration of the ramped part (angled bonnet section) of the hood. This example shows the details for such a ramped hood that will stand alone (the two adjacent cabinets will not intersect the hood.) In this type of design, it is typically recommended that there is at least 3 inches of clear wall space from the outside edge of the hood to the side of the cabinet.

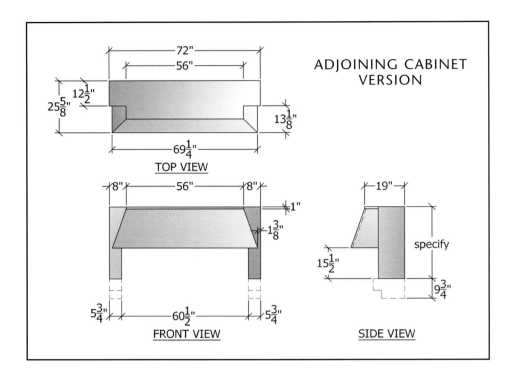

Figure 3.29 *The overall size of supporting elements.*

In this view, the hood is squared off so the cabinets can adjoin it. Do not leave this type of detailing as a jobsite decision.

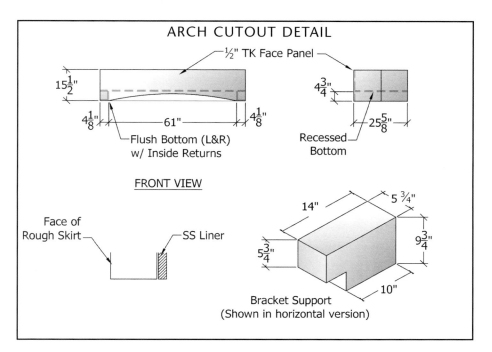

ARCH CUTOUT DETAIL

½" TK Face Panel

$15\frac{1}{2}$"

$4\frac{1}{8}$" | 61" | $4\frac{1}{8}$"

Flush Bottom (L&R)
w/ Inside Returns

$4\frac{3}{4}$"

$25\frac{5}{8}$"

Recessed
Bottom

FRONT VIEW

Face of
Rough Skirt

SS Liner

14"

$5\frac{3}{4}$"

$5\frac{3}{4}$"

$9\frac{3}{4}$"

10"

Bracket Support
(Shown in horizontal version)

TIPS FROM THE MASTERS

While drawings and details are better understood when professionally rendered as seen here, designers who supply CAD drawings that do not allow for this type of detail should note that even a crude hand sketch can—and usually does—provide the installer with the intent of the design. The designer also needs to clearly communicate the positions of stacked or combined mouldings to the installer to avoid much angst and confusion on the part of all parties. When in doubt, draw it out, even if it is a little squiggly.

Figure 3.30 *The relationship of the bracket supports, decorative walls and mantel hood.*
Engineer the exact size of the arched cut-out detail and the interior space of the hood so that you can order the custom stainless steel liner. Additionally, detail the exact sizing of the bracket supports so that the fabricating source (probably different from the source for the plaster decorative elements) can create these pieces in the correct dimensions.

CHECKLISTS TO HELP
YOU MANAGE THE
INSTALLATION

To avoid costly and time-consuming errors during installation, use these checklists to troubleshoot your projects upfront.

APPLIANCE CHECKLIST

Use the Appliance Checklist as you complete the final specifications for each kitchen project you work on. It will help you estimate and specify all the planning details of appliance placement.

Refrigerator Installation Considerations

1. Required door swing/drawer opening dimension verified. _____

2. Overall appliance depth (including air space and handles) listed on plans. _____

3. Overall width, including air space and countertop overhang dimension, determined before overhead cabinet width, size and height specified. _____

4. Appliance doors drawn in an open position on the plan to verify walkway clearances. _____

5. Ice maker copper water lines/water filter specified. _____

6. Trim kits and/or panels have been ordered. Labor to install has been included in estimate. _____

7. Special handles ordered for integrated units. _____

8. Location of power supply/outlets verified. _____

Dishwasher Installation Considerations

1. Trim kits and/or panels have been ordered. Labor to install has been included in estimate. _____

2. Existing water lines and drain location to be reused. _____

   New water line to be installed. _____

3. Existing dishwasher circuit to be reused. _____

   New dishwasher circuit to be added. _____

4. Appliance door drawn in an open position on the plan to verify walkway clearances. _____

5. How to secure appliance to stone countertop identified. _____

Trash Compactor Installation Considerations

1. Trim kits and/or panels have been ordered. Labor to install has been included in estimate. _____

2. Existing compactor circuit to be reused. _____

   New compactor circuit to be added. _____

3. Appliance door drawn in an open position on the plan to verify walkway clearances. _____

APPLIANCE CHECKLIST

Food Waste Disposer Installation Considerations

1. Unit to be batch feed _____ or continuous feed (switch) operated _____.   _____
2. Switch location located after considering primary user's handedness.   _____
   Wall location   _____
   Countertop location   _____
3. Waste line no higher than 17 inches on center off the floor.   _____

Backsplash Convenience Appliance Installation Considerations

1. Backsplash appliance does not interfere with wall stud placement.   _____
2. Recess required for appliance is not obstructed by vents, ducts or pocket doors.   _____
3. Recessed convenience appliances do not interfere with backsplash design or use.   _____
4. Convenience outlets along backsplash do not interfere with built-in backsplash appliance location.   _____
5. Heat generating backsplash appliances are not specified below task lighting that features a plastic diffuser.   _____

Drop-in, Slide-in or Free-standing Range Installation Considerations

1. Gas or electrical requirements:

   Gas   Size of existing gas line.   _____
            Existing gas line to be reused in its existing location.   _____
            Existing gas line to be relocated.   _____
            Diameter of new gas line required.   _____
            Gas regulator (shut off valve) located.   _____

   Electric   Electrical amperage of existing line:
            30 amp _____ 40 amp _____ 50 amp _____
            Electrical amperage requirement of new appliance:
            30 amp _____ 40 amp _____ 50 amp _____
            Existing electrical line to be reused in its existing location.   _____
            Existing electrical line to be relocated.   _____
            New electrical line to be added.   _____

2. Ventilation system specified on plans.   _____
3. Drop-in range method of support and distance from floor to bottom of range specified on plans.   _____
4. Countertop cut-out for drop-in units specified on plans.   _____
5. Side clearance for drop-in units which have a flange overlapping adjacent cabinetry has been considered in the planning process.   _____
6. Appliance overall depth, including handles, listed on the plans.   _____
7. Appliance door drawn in an open position to verify walkway clearances.   _____

APPLIANCE CHECKLIST

Built-in Oven Installation Considerations

1. Gas or electrical requirements:

Gas   Size of existing gas line. _____

Existing gas line to be reused in its existing location. _____

Existing gas line to be relocated. _____

Diameter of new gas line required. _____

Electric   Electrical amperage of existing line:

30 amp _____   40 amp _____   50 amp _____

Electrical amperage requirement of new appliance:

30 amp _____   40 amp _____   50 amp _____

Existing electrical line to be reused in its existing location. _____

Existing electrical line to be relocated. _____

New electrical line to be added. _____

2. Ventilation requirement for new oven: Ducted _____ Non-ducted _____

3. Countertop overhang treatment against oven cabinet side to be:

Countertop extends past oven case. _____

Countertop ties into side of special depth oven cabinet. _____

Case depth to be _____

Toekick to be _____

4. All dimensions are included in specifications and plans.

Overall appliance depth (including handles). _____

Appliance height placement in relationship to primary cook's height. _____

Cut-out and overall dimensions. _____

5. For under-counter installation, manufacturer's specifications have been verified _____
for minimum cut-out height from the floor.

Cooktop Installation Considerations

1. Gas or electrical requirements:

Gas   Size of existing gas line. _____

Existing gas line to be recessed in its present location. _____

Existing gas line to be relocated. _____

Diameter of new gas line required. _____

Electric   Electrical amperage of existing line:

30 amp _____   40 amp _____   50 amp _____

Electrical amperage requirement of new appliance:

30 amp _____   40 amp _____   50 amp _____

Existing electrical line to be reused in its existing location. _____

Existing electrical line to be relocated. _____

New electrical line to be added. _____

APPLIANCE CHECKLIST

Cooktop Installation Considerations (Continued)

2. Ventilation system specified on plans.   _____

3. Can cabinet drawers be installed below the cooktop?   _____

4. Can roll-outs be installed below the cooktop?   _____

5. All dimensions (cut-out and overall) are listed on the plan.   _____

Microwave Oven Installation Considerations

1. Dedicated electrical circuit specified.   _____

2. Trim kit ordered with appliance.   _____

   Labor to install trim kit included in estimate.   _____

3. Microwave oven placement is away from other heat generating appliances. _____

4. Microwave oven placement is away from television set in the kitchen.   _____

5. Appliance height has been determined in relation to the height of the primary cook   _____
   for both safety and convenience.

6. Cut-out and overall dimensions are listed on the plan.   _____

Ventilation Hood Installation Considerations

1. Length of duct path from ventilation system to exterior termination point. _____

2. Number of elbow turns (maximum of 3) along duct path.   _____

3. Space between elbows (minimum of 12 inches).

4. Ventilating unit's (free air pressure) cfm rating.   _____

5. Determine the need for replacement air fan for 300 cfm+ units.   _____

6. Hood depth in relation to adjacent cabinetry.   _____

7. Hood distance from cooking surface.   _____

8. Hood width in relationship to cooktop width below.   _____

9. Fireproof wall surface, cabinet surface requirements met.   _____

CABINET ORDER CHECKLIST

Use this 8 step checklist to completely verify the accuracy of your plan and the correct interpretation of your design by the cabinet manufacturer.

1. Carefully reviewed design for planning errors. Cabinet design details often lead to profit leaks.   _____
   - Dimensioning too tightly.
   - Missing the fit of intersecting elements.
   - Creating an element without proper engineering.

2. Decorative hardware selected before placing the cabinet order.   _____

   - _____
   - _____
   - _____
   - _____
   - _____
   - _____
   - _____
   - _____
   - _____
   - _____

3. Cabinet specifications verified.   _____

4. All appliance selections made (whether you are supplying them or not) before the cabinet order is placed.   _____

5. All field dimensions checked.   _____

6. Floor plan and dimensioned elevations prepared.   _____

7. Order reviewed against the plan and elevations.   _____

8. When the acknowledgement arrives, take quiet time to review it thoroughly.   _____

FIXTURES AND FITTINGS CHECKLIST

Bathroom designs are as complex as kitchen ones. Use this checklist when reviewing the completeness of your specifications.

TIPS FROM THE MASTERS

- Remember that damage on dark colored fixtures is noticeable. Dark colored fixtures also need more frequent cleaning by the homeowner.

- Regardless of the color, clients must be educated on how to clean all the various surfaces in new bathroom fixtures, fittings and materials. Abrasive cleaners can never be used.

- Make sure clients understand that colors blend and complement one another—they never match. Do not promise a perfect "match" between a vitreous china water closet, a fiberglass bathtub, a solid surface integral bowl and a glazed subway tile shower surround.

- In hard water areas, clients need to understand they must wipe down each fixture after use.

Toilet/Water Closet Installation Considerations

1. Has the rough-in dimension been checked when an existing toilet is being reused? The standard is 12 inches today, but some old toilets have a 10 inch or 14 inch rough-in.   _____

2. Have you noted the correct supply line height behind the toilet? Low-profile toilets normally specify a supply line rough-in closer to the floor. This may interfere with your baseboard. Higher seats (ADA requirement) have a different rough-in specification.   _____

3. Have you checked the water supply line size required for the toilet?   _____

4. Have you verified the toilet's dimension from the back wall to the front edge of the seat —comparing it with any door swings? In some small powder rooms this can be a critical dimension if you are attempting to use an elongated bowl.   _____

5. Have you verified the toilet paper holder is not being installed against a wall or recessed into a wall that has a pocket door?   _____

Bidet/Urinal Installation Considerations

1. Have you included a storage shelf or hooks for towels, soaps and other aids the user will require?   _____

2. Is there a robe hook close by to hang garments on?   _____

Lavatory/Vanity Cabinets Installation Considerations

1. Have you double-checked the faucet center set dimension against any predrilled lavatory specified?   _____

2. Have you located on the plan the exact rough-in for the supply and drain lines when using a specially designed cabinet or a pedestal?   _____

3. Have you located the exact placement for a wall-mounted faucet being used with a vessel bowl?   _____

4. Has the plumber been given "cut sheets" for any special cabinet that has specific rough-in requirements for the supply and water lines?   _____

125

FITTINGS AND FIXTURES CHECKLIST   Page 2 of 2

Lavatory/Vanity Cabinets Installation Considerations (Continued)

5. If the vanity is an off-the-floor unit, does the plumber know this? Remember, plumbers need to literally "crawl into" the vanity cavity to connect the water lines—can your plumber physically access the pipes in a specialty cabinet you are using?   _____

6. When using a shallow vanity cabinet (less than 21 inches deep), have you checked the overall lavatory depth (including the overflow channel) to make sure it will fit in the cabinet? Have you verified where the deck-mounted faucet will go in such a limited space installation? It may need to be placed left or right, not directly behind the bowl.   _____

Lavatory (Sink) Installation Considerations

1 Number of lavatory holes and fitting placement has been specified on the plans.   _____

2. Method of securing lavatory to counter surface has been determined: _____
   Flat rim with stainless steel rim and clip installation.   _____
   Self-rimming lavatory, color of caulking to be used between lavatory and countertop specified.   _____
   Under-mounted lavatory.   _____
   Integral lavatory.   _____

Shower Installation Considerations

1. If considering a one-piece shower enclosure in a renovation project, are you sure it will fit through interior doors?   _____

2. If replacing a shower pan, are you sure the new pan's shower drain is in exactly the same drain location?   _____

3. Have you included a waterproof light fixture in the enclosure?   _____

4. If using swinging doors for the shower enclosure, have you drawn them open on your plan to make sure they do not hit a nearby toilet or vanity?   _____

5. If replacing a bathtub with large shower, have you discussed this with your plumber? The normal 1 1/2-inch tub drain may not be adequate for a stall shower, which typically requires a 2-inch drain.   _____

Bathtub Installation Considerations

1. Have you specified whether the tub is to be a left or right hand drain?   _____

2. If replacing an old tub, have you carefully checked the space? 66 inch x 30 inch tubs are sometimes found in older installations and will require additional work to modify the space to receive the more common 60-inch x 32-inch or 60-inch x 34-inch fixture.   _____

3. Have you ordered a new waste and overflow?   _____

4. Did you specify the correct waste and overflow for that specific tub?   _____

5. Have you planned on how your installation crew is going to protect the tub once installed?   _____

6. For an oversized tub being installed on a second or third level (or even in the basement) of a home, during a jobsite visit have you thought through how you will get the tub in-place?   _____

JOBSITE CHECKLIST

Use this checklist to review all the materials specified for the project, as well as a final "are we ready" list of jobsite preparation concerns.

Project Name_____   Project No. _____
Address _____   Date _____
City, State, Zip _____

Client/Design Information

1. Have all job data, including name, address, job location, directions. _____
2. Have assigned a job number. _____
3. Have complete design drawings, including floor plan and elevations:
   All dimensions are in inches and fractions of an inch or in metric sizing. _____
   All overall dimensions total equal individual wall segment dimensions. _____
   Wall heights are indicated. _____
   If no soffit, installed wall cabinet heights are indicated. _____
   Allowances are made for out-of-square corners. _____
   Special dimensions for peninsula and island placement are noted. _____

Jobsite Special Conditions/Conflicts

1. Out-of-square and out-of-plumb corners and walls are noted. _____
2. Flooring conditions that may affect cabinet installation noted. _____
3. Conflicts between electrical receptacles/switches and cabinets and/or backsplash decorative material noted. _____
4. Conflicts with phone jacks noted. _____
5. HVAC supplies and returns noted. _____
6. Plumbing fixture centerlines located. _____
7. Door and window casings located with widths noted. _____
8. Supply line for ice maker located. _____
9. Power/gas line for range and wall ovens located. _____

Cabinetry and Layout

1. NKBA Guidelines followed to greatest extent feasible. _____
2. Base cabinet and wall cabinet individual dimensions correspond to overall total dimension. _____
3. Fillers provided where necessary for door and drawer clearances. _____
4. Fillers provided at 90-degree inside corners. _____
5. Proper door hinging provided. _____
6. Any special conditions or cabinet modifications provided. _____
7. Finished ends at wall cabinets noted. _____
8. Finished ends at base cabinets noted. _____
9. Clearances between full overlay doors/drawers and mouldings adequate. _____
10. Clearances between full overlay doors/drawers and baseboards adequate. _____
11. Pulls for any special base cabinets noted. _____
12. Pulls for any special wall cabinets noted. _____
13. Allowance provided for waste in moulding installation. _____
14. Adequate clearances provided for aligning tall cabinets. _____

JOBSITE CHECKLIST   Page 2 of 2

Island/Peninsula Cabinets
1. Cabinet dimensions are adequate. _____
2. Framed half-wall, if used, is properly sized, with mouldings and panels noted. _____
3. Outside corner detailed. _____
4. Scribe locations noted and method provided for. _____
5. Toekick detailed. _____
6. Paneling for exposed sides noted. _____
7. Cabinet orientation indicated, if non-standard. _____
8. Locations of built-in switches indicated. _____
9. Any other special conditions noted. _____

Countertops
1. Lengths verified with base cabinets. _____
2. Overhang dimension noted at open ends and adjacent to specific appliances. _____
3. Raised sections indicated with method of support detailed. _____
4. Lowered sections indicated with method of support detailed. _____
5. Special conditions have been fully detailed in design drawings. _____
6. Backsplash locations indicated, and fit and finish noted regarding end caps and splash/deck joint. _____
7. Radius and/or angled corners are dimensioned. _____
8. Edge treatments described. _____
9. Cutouts located by centerline and dimensioned. _____

Appliances
1. Appliance specification cut sheets available. _____
2. Clearances between appliances and cabinet doors/drawers specified. _____
3. Downdraft ducting provided for. _____
4. Exhaust ducting for vent hoods provided for. _____
5. Dishwasher clearances adequate. _____
6. Range clearances adequate. _____
7. Cooktop dimensions verified with countertop. _____
8. Wall oven dimensions coordinated with cabinet. _____
9. Disposal located, with respect to the side of sink, and switch location noted. _____
10. Microwave specified and located. _____
11. Refrigerator specified and located. _____

Glass Shelving/Counter Section/Cabinet Doors or Other Special Decorative Material
1. Type, location and sizes indicated. _____
2. Quantities scheduled. _____

Hardware
1. Quantity indicated allows for two extra (for contingencies or to give to owner). _____
2. Clearances required at 90-degree inside corners verified with cabinet fillers. _____

_____   _____
                 Signature   Date

CHAPTER 4: The Installation Team

Historically, the kitchen and bathroom industry consists of four segments:

- Manufacturers
- Product Representatives and Distributors
- Retailers, Dealers and Designers
- Contractors, Installation Specialists and Specific Trades People

Their interaction and respective functions constitute the delivery system that provides kitchen and bathroom products and services.

The success or failure of a project depends on how closely the various segments work together to support one another and drive their mutual success.

In our industry it is an accepted fact that the consumer's decision to buy from you is based on both the products you represent and the quality and efficiency of the installation services you provide or recommend. If your installation department is unstructured or poorly trained, this can be the weakest link in your delivery system and in your success in this industry. If the installation process is unnecessarily long, the workmanship poor or the jobsite messy, the client will not be happy with any part of the project. When clients are unhappy with the condition of the jobsite or quality of the work, they will, oftentimes, blame the products and/or the kitchen designer who sold them the products, rather than realizing the issue is one related to installation.

TYPES OF INSTALLATIONS

There are four major types of projects in our industry:
- Replacement
- Remodeling
- Room Addition/Tear-down/Build-around Projects
- New Construction

Replacement

A kitchen or bath replacement usually involves minimal changes in an existing design. An existing layout remains intact, and new products are installed. A replacement might include refacing existing cabinets and installing new appliances, countertops and decorative surfaces. Or a replacement might include upgrades in the cabinet quality, layout or quantity, with all mechanical elements remaining in existing locations.

Remodeling

A remodeling project usually includes a new design for the space. A remodel generally requires new plumbing, electrical and mechanical systems. It may include structural changes, such as wall removal, additions, or the installation of new doors and windows. This type of project requires building permits. A remodeling project requires the greatest amount of design and technical skills, management knowledge and communication expertise on the part of the designer.

Room Addition/Tear-down/Build-around Projects

An emerging trend in the building industry combines remodeling work with new construction in the form of a major structural addition to an existing house, or the partial/complete teardown of an existing structure that results in a new home. This type of project is very different from new construction because it involves working in a mature neighborhood—not in a new subdivision or converting open land to a residential community.

Three key design criteria for such a project are the ability to join the new structure to the existing structure, the knowledge to meet existing building codes, and the skill to work within mechanical constraints when adding new construction to an existing home.

New Construction

Typically, new construction is led by the builder if the home is built "on speculation"—meaning there is no owner at the time of groundbreaking. In the case of a new custom home, the owner and/or the agent (architect, build/design professional, interior designer) controls the specification process.

INSTALLATION SERVICE BUSINESS MODELS

There are many different successful business models that relate to the installation portion of the project. Each of these models affects a designer's jobsite responsibilities, communication with field personnel and accountability for errors or omissions discovered at the jobsite once the installation process begins.

These business models are defined by who manages the job.

Business Model No. 1: A design firm with an employed project manager acting as a liaison between the designer and field personnel

A project manager frees up the designer's time to focus on new sales. This business model can also let each individual focus on what they do best—design or organize. On the negative side, adding a project manager to the staff increases the overhead of the firm. And, with one more person involved on the job the likelihood of communication breakdowns occurring between the designer of record and the project manager increases. The biggest omission is often details about the project that the designer is aware of (because of the many conversations with the client) that are not easily transferred to the project manager. It is also possible the clients will "disconnect" as they learn they are no longer dealing with "their" designer.

Business Model No. 2: A design firm without a project manager, the designer manages the installation and directs all field personnel

A designer who shepherds the project from concept to completion serves the client well because small details resulting from conversation will not be lost. The client also benefits from working with the designer on an on-going basis because jobsite trauma can be stabilized as the emotional roller coaster goes on. However, this type of arrangement puts the responsibility for detail-oriented project management squarely on the designer's shoulders. Eliminating the added overhead of a project manager might seem like saving money, but this can only be determined when the firm carefully evaluates the actual percentage of profit generated at the conclusion of the

Business Model No. 4: A design firm that does not provide any installation services other than referrals to installation specialists

The firm offers a referral list of recommended installation specialists who report directly to the client and are retained under a separate contract. The designer remains accountable for the finished product and is typically expected to have an oversight responsibility.

This business model is typical on new construction projects, where the kitchen designer is simply one of many suppliers to the builder providing casework for specific rooms in the home. The builder's trim carpenters, oftentimes, are expected to install the cabinetry.

Business Model No. 5: A design firm that does not offer installation services and does not recommend installation specialists

The design firm's responsibility is completed with delivery of the components.

This business model works well for simpler projects and for firms serving a skillful do-it-yourself client base or a contractor who has a long history of working with the firm. This arrangement is not successful on complex projects, or for a firm whose plans and specifications are typically riddled with errors, omissions or inaccuracies.

Regardless of the designer's responsibility during installation seasoned experts suggest that making sure the jobsite construction, HVAC and mechanicals are "as per plan" is time well spent. Additionally, with today's technology, extending channels of communication via digital photographs, cell phone calls from the jobsite, or video conferencing with a laptop from the jobsite can increase the potential for success.

KEY COMPETENCIES OF INSTALLATION SPECIALISTS

Seasoned professionals recommend finding an installer who possesses:

- *A complete understanding of the local municipality permitting process and building codes.* The installation specialist must be able to communicate with inspectors onsite, understand the permit posting requirements and be knowledgeable regarding construction building codes.

- *A basic knowledge of kitchen and bathroom design.* While not actually required to do the complete design, installers need to master the principles of design so that they can make decisions in the field and communicate effectively with the designer.

- *A thorough understanding of carpentry skills.* Installers need a base of knowledge and experience in carpentry covering everything related to the construction of a shell, including constructing stud walls and other framing; installing doors and windows and the construction of openings for these doors and windows; blocking required for cabinet and fixture installation; and general finish trim requirements.

- *Specific and detailed knowledge of cabinet and countertop construction and installation.* These skills include everything from field measurement and survey work to actual layout and cabinet and equipment installation.

- *Familiarity with finish materials.* Installers work in tandem with other trades. Therefore, they need to understand the installation techniques for each of these materials and their impact on the cabinet and fixture installation.

- *A thorough understanding of all of the appliances and equipment items.* Installers need to understand standard installation and mounting techniques for these items, as well as electrical, plumbing and ventilation requirements.

- *Techniques for ceiling construction.* Installers must understand ceiling framing systems and know how to install ceiling joists and how to frame soffits in preparation for drywall, plaster or other finishes.

- *A basic knowledge of mechanical systems.* Installers need to be familiar with the following mechanical systems: electrical, plumbing, gas, heating and ventilation, air-conditioning and cooking equipment ventilation. A good, basic knowledge of all of the mechanical systems gives the installer the knowledge necessary to efficiently plan and sequence the work of the various mechanical trades.

- *Adherence to jobsite safety.* In order to protect both people and property, installers need a clear understanding of established safety rules and procedures and the most effective way to carry out these recommendations.

- *Excellent people skills.* To deal effectively with clients, installers must be able to get along with people. This includes establishing comfortable relationships with clients, and working well with others involved in the installation process.

- *An appreciation for the importance of pre-installation conferences.* A pre-installation conference helps everyone clearly understand the specifics of the job.

- *The practice of good jobsite management.* An understanding of, and adherence to, effective staging and sequencing is extremely important to ensure that the job finishes in a timely and efficient manner.

- *A good mechanical aptitude, and a clear understanding of how to maintain tools and equipment.* Although a cabinet installer first, the installer should also have good general mechanical ability. This includes a familiarity with all types of tools and equipment and how to keep this equipment in good working condition.

- *Familiarity with the legal issues.* Installers must be aware of liabilities at the jobsite and have a clear understanding of responsibilities before the work begins.

- *A clear understanding of installation and construction terms.* The complex nature of this profession requires installers to be familiar with a wide array of terms used by installers and the other related trades working on the jobsite.

- *Have the ability to read design plans.*

DEVELOPING A SUCCESSFUL WORKING RELATIONSHIP WITH YOUR TRADE PARTNERS AND INSTALLERS

Relationship Between the Designer and a Subcontractor/Trade Partner

The best working relationships between a designer and a trade partner rely on a trade agreement, with a firm estimate provided at time of proposal preparation, and a jobsite inspection sheet signed before the crews leave the job. Although some firms offer incentives to their trade partners, many do not. However, what all firms speak of is the importance of respect.

Successful kitchen and bath designers actively engage their trade contractors as business partners with clear, regular and scheduled communication, shared educational opportunities, and an agreed-to set of performance guidelines and expectations.

To insure there are no surprises, an agreement between the firm and the trade partners addresses:

- Licensing and insurance.
- Job safety and OSHA requirements.
- Onsite attire.

  1. Wear professional carpenter pants, not jogging sweats or jeans.

  2. Always wear a shirt. Sleeveless t-shirts, shirts with offensive phrases or logos are not allowed. It is highly recommended the design firm encourage some type of uniform for the installation team, whether it is a generic recommendation for types of shoes, pants and shirts, or a uniform for employees.

  3. Footwear: Recommend flat soles, as opposed to waffle-bottom or hiking shoes, to minimize tracking in dirt and mud. Alternatively, separate shoes for indoor and outdoor work are worthwhile. No sandals or beach shoes permitted.

  4. All vehicles will be clean and in good condition. Leaking motor oil or transmission fluid on the client's driveway is unacceptable.

- Behavior when on the jobsite.

  1. No smoking.

  2. Radios require prior agreement with client on volume and music choice.

  3. No profanity.

  4. No eating in any part of the house—other than the work area. In nice weather, seek permission from the client to sit outside.

  5. No flirting—with anybody!

  6. No non-work related chattering.

  7. No discussions about any delicate topics: religion, politics, etc.

  8. No extensive personal conversations via PDA, e-mail or phone while on the jobsite.

9. Do not possess, sell, trade or offer for sale illegal drugs or alcohol, or otherwise engage in the illegal use of drugs or alcohol on the jobsite.

10. Only use the restroom assigned to the project.

11. Never place any tools and/or equipment on any finished surfaces.

12. Maintain a neat and clean jobsite at all times.

Relationship Between the Designer and the Installer

Experienced professionals suggest the following foundation points in developing a good relationship with the installer.

- Your goal is to make the installer's job as easy as possible. Similarly, the installer believes their primary goal is to make the designer look good.

- Leave egos at the door. You should include the installer in a design review and any "what should we do?" discussions. Installers should never negatively comment (verbally or non-verbally) about the designer and/or the designer's work to the client.

- A communication system exists between you and the installer that includes the client when appropriate or takes place away from the client when appropriate.

- Both the designer and installer are readily available to one another via telephone, beeper or e-mail as needed.

- The designer includes the installer in praises given for a job well done: sharing photographs of complete projects, or inviting the installation team to celebrations at the jobsite are just several small ways of sharing the finished project with these hardworking professionals.

WHAT SHOULD THE INSTALLER PROMISE THE DESIGNER?

- Carry the necessary liability insurance and follow proper tax laws as instructed by their accountants.

- Communicate effectively in the English language and to be able to review the contractual documents, the plans and specifications, directions to the jobsite and other notes as they relate to a job.

- Manage the upkeep of the jobsite workbook as instructed by the design firm/designer. Accept, inspect and safely store any material delivered directly to the jobsite.

- Immediately contact the project manager or the designer if any unexpected construction constraints are identified—if the client requests any additional work, if there are any product oversights, mishaps or other problems identified that require reorder. Where appropriate, these materials will be maintained in an agreed-to punchlist format.

- Not to perform any work requested by the client without a signed change order.

- Maintain a proper, professional appearance, respect the client's neighborhood, property and home; refrain from loud talking, smoking, foul language, playing loud music, or any other activity the client deems disruptive or unprofessional on the jobsite.

- If design modifications need to be discussed, contact the designer/project manager away from the client to facilitate a private conversation.

- Provide scheduling for jobsite inspections, as necessary, pre-installation jobsite conferences, and completion of punchlist items as per the design firm's agreement.

- Submit invoices as agreed to with the design firm on a regular basis, listing all work performed.

- Provide warranty work on their portion of the project.

- Respect all other subcontractors and/or contract installers working on the jobsite.

- Lay out all work ahead of time, and stock all required materials required on trucks or vehicles to minimize time-consuming trips to a supply house.

- Maintain a pleasant, professional attitude with the client, avoiding any comment on the design, quality of the project and reputation of the firm/designer. Never answer questions posed by the owner or owner's agent regarding design details. Immediately refer the owner or owner's agent to the designer of record, or proactively arrange a meeting/telephone call/e-mail message to facilitate the proper dialog between the designer of record and the client.

WHAT SHOULD THE DESIGNER PROMISE THE INSTALLER?

- Prompt payment according to an agreed-upon schedule.

- Follow the jobsite workbook format and prepare the plans in a consistent way so that the installation team becomes accustomed to working with the same type of material.

- Share market strategies, the firm's business model, and make sure the individual is invited to see completed projects to instill a sense of confidence on the installer's part about the opportunity for a long-term working relationship with the firm.

- Provide clean, accurate plans, specifications and details.

- Never schedule the installer's time without an open dialog.

- Provide information about the client's personality before the installation specialists arrive at the jobsite.

- Maintain an established review process to evaluate mistakes when determining who is going to pay.

- Maintain a clear accounts payable process and stick to the agreed-upon payment schedule.

PRE-CONSTRUCTION CONFERENCE

This conference with clients is an absolute necessity, especially for kitchen and bathroom remodeling projects. Hold it onsite, immediately following the initial jobsite walk-through and include the client, retailer/dealer/designer, installer, and the production manager, where applicable.

At the conference, review the contract one more time to ensure that the client understands just what is, and is not, included. Because most clients have discussed a variety of options on a project, and compromises are often necessary to bring in a job on budget, it is easy for them to forget just what the specifications will be.

It is absolutely essential that the client make every selection for the project prior to or during the pre-construction conference. Many retailers/dealers/designers and installers also insist that all materials for the job be in stock or onsite before work begins.

This meeting passes the chain of command from the retailer/dealer/designer to the installer. If planning a lead installer model, make this clear to the client. They must understand that they will work with the lead installer rather than the designer. (If a client continues to call the retailer/dealer/designer during the course of the project, the lead installer will not be able to take full control of the project or gain the respect of the client.) Alternatively, the pre-construction conference gives the installation specialist an opportunity to thoroughly review the project with the designer and client.

If the company employs a production manager, the production manager can assist in the presentation of project details, eliminating some of the need for the installer to get involved. However, the installer must still attend at the pre-construction conference, and the production manager should stress to the client who will have ultimate responsibility for the day-to-day operation of the project.

In addition to instructing and explaining, an installer needs to listen. Most clients have one or two pet peeves that concern them most. One person might have concern about hammer marks on the trim, but be completely oblivious to whether or not the wall insulation is installed properly. Another person might be concerned about air leakage or energy conservation. This does not mean that clients should set the standard of quality for an installer, but it is advantageous to know what areas should receive extra care and attention if a client is to be satisfied.

The pre-construction conference establishes the line of communication between the firm, the installer and client. Good communication skills are very important to the success of the project.

Where there is more than one client, designate just one person to be the key decision maker and liaison to the firm's responsible project manager. This person should be responsible for handling payments and for initiating change orders.

TIPS FROM THE MASTERS:
Sample Topics for Pre-Construction Conference

- If there is a garage on the premises, set aside at least one bay for storage and staging of cabinetry, appliances, fixtures and finishing materials.

- If there will be interior work, decide where the client's furniture, rugs, curtains, etc., will be stored. Discuss dust protection of adjoining rooms and disruption of the rest of the house. Advise that if a household member is allergic to dust, other living arrangements might be made. Alternatively, the allergic person might move to a room on a floor unaffected by construction.

- When a kitchen is gutted and remodeled, there will be no working sink or appliances or even counter space. Find out where to temporarily locate the refrigerator. Arrange to loan a hot plate and/or microwave oven to the client. Does the client wish to keep the removed cabinets or will they be hauled away? (If the cabinets are of the old, built-in-place type, which do not remove in one piece, make this clear to the client.) Give the client a clear picture of what will and will not be removed from the existing kitchen, and what the completed space will look like. Also impress upon the client the importance of emptying cabinets and removing all valuable items prior to the start of the project.

- If a wall will be removed between the existing house and a new bump-out or addition, the timing of wall removal is of utmost importance to the client. Most installers try to enclose the bump-out or addition before tearing out, but this is not always possible. Keep the client informed about when the tear-out will occur. Opening up an existing house is just a construction project for an installer, but it is a heating, air conditioning, privacy, housekeeping and security issue to the client.

- Point out that any required matching (floor tiles, special moulding, windows, doors, etc.) will match "as closely as possible from stock materials at existing local sources of supply." Even this phrase is subject to misunderstanding. Inform clients of potential major differences and encourage them to visit the supplier or view samples of what is available.

- Discuss everything, even the placement of electrical outlets. If the installer is working with designer—(or architect)—plans, all outlets should be shown and specified but should still be reviewed. Exact placement of outlets is important where appliances need to be connected, or where the outlets are integrated into a tile backsplash with a pattern.

- Decide where to position a suspended light fixture. Will the junction box be centered on a bay window, the space, or to the anticipated location of a table? Electricians and installers often make this decision without consulting the client, leading to unexpected costs of moving it later, including a separate trip by the electrician, drywaller and painter. "Who will pay for this?" can be a difficult discussion.

TIPS FROM THE MASTERS –
Sample Topics for Pre-Construction Conference continued

- Many clients have strong feelings about certain small details, and they tend to assume that everyone working on the project shares their feelings. They also assume the right installer will ask the right questions and make the right judgments. Examples include silent switches, type of dimmer, use of stainless or white plastic outlet cover plates in the kitchen, and a ceramic towel rack in the tub area (or never in the tub area). A client may plan to stain all trim and be astonished to find that the trim is finger-jointed. Needless to say, there is no way that the installation team, designer of record or the project manager can cover every area. However, close attention to past experiences, client comments and the client's present living style are helpful in providing clues to areas of possible confusion or misunderstanding.

- For a bath remodel, make the client aware that there will be three or four days during which it will be unusable. Assure the client of adequate notice and minimal downtime, but fairness and good business practice dictate a clear understanding. The client should also understand that at the end of the three- or four-day period, the bathroom will be usable, but not finished.

- When installing a bathroom on the second floor directly over a bathroom on the first floor, the plumber will have to tie-in below the sink on the first floor. This requires opening up and patching the wall and painting the room or the affected wall. If only the wall is painted, it may or may not match the existing paint in the room. If this is not clarified, costs to repaint the entire room will be the subject of another unpleasant discussion about "who will pay for this?"

- Suggest changing all the accessible piping in a home with galvanized pipes to copper, CPVC or PEX during construction. Point out that galvanized pipes rust from the inside out and ultimately clog. As the rust increases, the aperture gets smaller. When installing a new bath using the same horizontal galvanized pipes, there will be a noticeable drop in water pressure if more than one fixture is turned on. If you do not explain this, the client may, understandably, accuse the installation team of ruining the water pressure in the house and expect it to be corrected.

Each of these points—only a few of many possible misunderstandings—illustrates the compelling need for a pre-construction conference. Forewarned is forearmed, and so a conference is a key part of a successful installation delivery system.

THE JOBSITE "BIBLE"

To insure clear communication and to minimize down time, prepare a project binder which remains at the jobsite at all times.

The NKBA book *Kitchen & Bath Business Management* includes a list of items to place in a document package to keep in a book on the project site. They include:

- A map and written directions to jobsite. Gate access information, if necessary.

- Contract scope, omitting financial details.

- Construction calendar.

- Homeowner target dates for open selections.

- Salvage report listing what to keep and where to put it.

- Subcontractor list, with contact information and job scope details.

- Cut sheets of materials, specifications, install sheets, product warranties.

- Salesperson and homeowner's contact information, with e-mail addresses and 24-hour emergency contact information.

- Plans and elevations.

- Permit and inspection reports.

- Miscellaneous, such as receipts for homeowners.

- Change order request forms.

- Place for checks from homeowner.

CHAPTER 5: The Business of Design: Estimating the Project and Developing the Specifications

In some businesses, the designer is responsible for gathering all costs and estimates from subcontractors, as well as proposals from countertop suppliers and cabinet estimate costs, and then applying the company's agreed to markup to the final contract documents. In other firms, a separate department prepares cost information and the contractual documents and the designer's responsibility is presenting the proposal to the client and gaining their acceptance.

The NKBA book *Kitchen & Bath Business Management* offers an in-depth discussion of the pricing formulas used to develop a profit plan. It is so critical that designers understand the basic elements of pricing that the information appears again here.

Regardless of the firm's business model, the most important thing to understand is that it is not the designer's prerogative to change the firm's profit planning process.

Figure 5.1 *A diagram of Standard Markups.* (Courtesy of Hank Darlington)

Standard Markup: A standard markup is the multiplier amount (often expressed as a percentage) of the original cost you are adding to the cost to determine the sell price required to produce the gross profit your business is based on. For example, assume your desired markup is "Y":

Cost x Markup = Sell	$12,000 Cabinet Order
Y = 0.0% $100 x **1.00** = $100	$12,000 x **1.00** = $12,000
Y =33.0% $100 x **1.50** = $150	$12,000 x **1.50** = $18,000
Y =37.5% $100 x **1.60** = $160	$12,000 x **1.60** = $19,200
Y =39.0% $100 x **1.65** = $165	$12,000 x **1.65** = $19,800
Y =42.0% $100 x **1.72** = $172	$12,000 x **1.72** = $20,640

Gross Profit to Price: You can determine what the sell price would be, given a particular profit, by using this formula:

$$\text{Selling Price} = \frac{\text{Cost of Goods or Services} \times 100}{100\% - \text{Gross Profit }\%}$$

For instance, if a cabinet set costs $12,000 and your desired gross profit is 42%, you would calculate the selling price as follows:

Example #1: $12,000 Cabinets - 42% Gross Profit

$$\text{Selling Price} = \frac{\$12,000 \times 100 = \$1,200,000}{100 - 42 = 58} = \$20,690$$

Example #2: $12,000 Cabinets - 39% Gross Profit

$$\text{Selling Price} = \frac{\$12,000 \times 100 = \$1,200,000}{100 - 39 = 61} = \$19,672$$

Example #3: $12,000 Cabinets - 36% Gross Profit

$$\text{Selling Price} = \frac{\$12,000 \times 100 = \$1,200,000}{100 - 36 = 64} = \$18,750$$

Example #4: $12,000 Cabinets - 33% Gross Profit

$$\text{Selling Price} = \frac{\$12,000 \times 100 = \$1,200,000}{100 - 33 = 67} = \$17,910$$

Price to Gross Profit: If you are considering a particular price and want to know what the amount of your gross profit would be, you can figure that out, too:

$$\text{Gross Profit} = \frac{\text{Selling Price - Cost}}{\text{Selling Price}}$$

Using the cost and selling price from the previous examples, the gross profit would be calculated like this.

Example #1: $\dfrac{\$20,690 - \$12,000}{\$20,690} = 42\%$

Example #2: $\dfrac{\$19,672 - \$12,000}{\$19,672} = 39\%$

Example #3: $\dfrac{\$18,750 - \$12,000}{\$18,750} = 36\%$

Example #4: $\dfrac{\$17,910 - \$12,000}{\$17,910} = 33\%$

PRICING STRATEGIES

There are three broad pricing strategies used in the kitchen and bath industry:

- **Lump-Sum Pricing**: The client gets one price for the project without listing items individually.

  Lump-sum pricing should be carefully detailed with all allowances noted so the clients know exactly what they are buying.

  Even if using a lump-sum contract, include a time-and-materials-price to cover all unknown construction problems (such as dry rot).

- **Cost-Plus Pricing**: Each cost is identified and followed by an agreed to markup factor. Normally, a not-to-exceed total is established.

  Cost-plus pricing is effective on jobs plagued with many change orders. Caution: The client may feel dissatisfied knowing the size of the firm's markup.

  When using cost-plus pricing add a contingency factor that is based on the historical performance of the estimator, salesperson or company specialist. Therefore, if an individual's past estimate numbers have not been accurate, adding a 2% to 5% "slippage" factor makes sense.

- **Time and Material Pricing**: No final total cost is identified. Invoice the costs (plus an agreed to markup factor) according to an agreed schedule.

The majority of specialists in the kitchen and bath industry agree that *lump-sum pricing* is the best way to build a profitable company with a satisfied client base. Use *cost-plus pricing* and *time-and-materials pricing* for projects when unknowns can potentially lead to higher costs.

PRICING METHODS

Unit Pricing

The unit price method (also known as the "piece method") requires the company's management assign a value to each installation operation or piece of material. For example, each cabinet or foot of moulding or miter cut carries a dollar point or value. A total is simple addition if a dollar value is used. Add points up and then multiply by an established value.

Unit pricing works well in the replacement market. It is harder to apply this method if there is a great deal of variation in cabinet configuration or architectural accoutrements and mouldings used on the project.

Linear-Foot Pricing

Use the linear foot pricing method to quote a preliminary budget. Linear-foot pricing is not as accurate as the other systems. Based on historical data, assign a linear-foot price to base and wall cabinets with counters and/or tall cabinets.

Custom Quotation Method (Sometimes Called "The Stick Method")

Although it's the most time-consuming, the custom quotation method is also the most accurate. Use this pricing on a plan review or jobsite visit, and a complete detailing of a material list as well as a per-project labor estimate of the time required to complete the project. All costs for material, labor, permits, professional fees, clean-up and trash disposal are then added to identify a hard cost and the profit margin is applied.

PROTECTING
YOUR PROFITS

Unfortunately, there are common mistakes made in project estimating or project production that result in profit slippage.

Three Major Causes of Profit Slippage

1. Material Slippage

   • Insufficient quantity of materials delivered to the site.

   • Material price increases.

   • Damaged materials delivered to the site.

2. Labor/Subcontractor/Sales Slippage

   • Production errors and/or product ordering errors.

   • Poor job management by production manager or lead installer (carpenter).

   • Not securing bids from subcontractors: working in an open-ended forum.

3. Contract/Client Slippage

   • Taking costly steps to please the client.

   • Numerous and undocumented change orders.

   • Unclear contract specifications.

Your Profits are Protected When

   • You know your firm's estimating practices and you stick to them.

   • Regardless of the costing system used, you give special consideration to projects that are outside the firm's normal product offering or design expertise, are a distance away from the firm's marketing area, or involve a client who may be difficult to work with or to satisfy.

   • You charge for the "hassle factor" for clients who may prove to be difficult.

   • You employ the concept of teamwork at critical points in the project.
      • Double-check jobsite dimensions.
      • Conduct a pre-job start conference.
      • Produce clear product orders.
      • Meeting with the client on an ongoing basis.

Judgment Factors in Estimating

It is clear that unit pricing has a number of advantages over other estimating methods. But even unit pricing cannot provide everything necessary to produce a complete and accurate estimate.

Prepare the basic estimate and then analyze the job for special requirements. Consider job conditions, any special features of the job itself, client requirements, company capabilities and code requirements.

CONDITION ANALYSIS

Examine the job for any variations from the standard that could be covered by a unit-pricing system. Special access problems, unusual existing conditions, etc. will greatly affect job costs and so they must get special attention during the estimating process. Examples of special conditions include, but are certainly not limited to, the following:

- If the installation is a bathroom on the third floor of a house and no windows are large enough to bring materials through, allow an additional cost for carrying materials upstairs. If the stairway is narrow and standard 4 foot x 8 foot sheets of drywall will not fit, there will be more costs to cut the sheets and install a greater number of pieces. If the crew must maneuver a large whirlpool tub or shower unit up the stairway, it will require extra time. Installers may even need to repaint the stairwell at the end of the job to repair damage caused during the course of the job.

- If the installation is located in a house on a hill with no driveway up to the house, there will be an additional cost to transport the materials up the hill.

- If work inside a house will be done near areas with light-colored carpeting, antique furniture, etc., there will be an additional cost for the special care necessary to avoid soiling or damaging the valuable items.

- The cost of painting varies greatly depending upon the amount of preparation that is necessary. If many old coats must be scraped off, or if wallpaper must be removed from plaster walls, which likely will involve plasterwork, the cost will be much higher than for painting a clean, bare surface.

- In some neighborhoods, parking is severely limited for trucks and other construction vehicles. When this problem is known to installers in advance, their estimate should reflect an extra cost for parking tickets, the cost of parking in a lot and, perhaps, additional time to get to and from a job.

- If the work day is restricted by building regulations, or if work is to be done only when the clients are away at work or in less time than would normally be expected, the estimate must cover any overtime or additional help to meet these requirements.

- If there are animals or small children who will be around while work is going on, there must be some additional cost to compensate for their intrusions and for the additional care required.

- Matching existing materials can be a problem, even if specifications are written to protect the installer from having to provide a perfect match between new and existing materials. The necessary materials may not be readily available, and transportation costs may be high, or there may be special charges for such things as custom millwork.

CLIENT ANALYSIS

Some clients are so difficult to work with that a profitable project is not possible. You need to know how to recognize these clients and how to deal with them—and you may need to walk away from them.

You need to recognize the types of people who are most likely to cause trouble. Smart designers learn to analyze clients and adjust their estimates upwards when there are signals of trouble ahead. Some examples include:

- If a client wants the estimate to itemize labor, materials, subcontract, overhead and profit, it usually means that the client will be very difficult to deal with. Many design firms simply refuse to do this, saying that they only give lump sum bids. At the very least, designers should be on notice with this type of client and estimate the job accordingly.

- If a client demands that the job be completed in an unreasonable time, and is planning a major social function or event in their home the day they want the project completed, designers can be assured that the relationship with this client will be extremely demanding and troublesome.

- Designers should be wary of a client who is continually negotiating for a better price during the estimating process. A client who is difficult during the early stages will probably be even more difficult as the job goes on.

- If you note that during the survey appointment a client seems to be extremely meticulous and intolerant of any disorder, they may have unrealistic expectations about the installation process which can cost the installer a lot of money.

- If there are two clients (a husband and wife, for example) who are in frequent disagreement during the early stages of the project, this should be a clear warning of how the decision-making process will occur during installation.

- Be alert to a client who insists on special order items for everything, rather than accepting products normally handled by the installer and retailer/dealer/designer. Special order items usually come from sources outside the design firm's normal supply lines, delivery is usually slow, and cash requirements are higher. Reflect these problems as an increase in the installer's markup.

Measurement Standards

Designers should be familiar with measuring standards they may be required to use during the estimating process. (Note that these are not the same as measuring standards used for creating project plans.)

Round all figures upward to the nearest even number. Most building materials are bought in 2-foot dimensions, so the materials will be the same for a 14-foot wide kitchen addition as for a 13-foot 6-inch addition, and there will be little or no difference in the labor.

Material quantities should also be rounded up to the nearest even number, not only because of 2 foot dimension increments, but because rounding allows for necessary waste. Also, if you use simple, even numbers, mistakes in arithmetic are less likely.

Figure all walls with window and door openings as solid because the slight savings on materials is more than offset by additional labor to cut around the openings.

The following basic formulas determine standard units of measure that installers typically work with. These include:

Figure 5.2 and 5.3 To calculate square footage, multiply length x width.

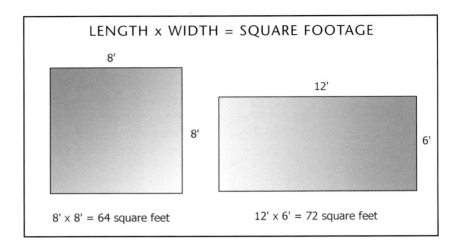

LENGTH x WIDTH = SQUARE FOOTAGE

8'

8'

12'

6'

8' x 8' = 64 square feet   12' x 6' = 72 square feet

Figure 5.4 To calculate square footage of a triangular area, multiply width x height x 1/2.

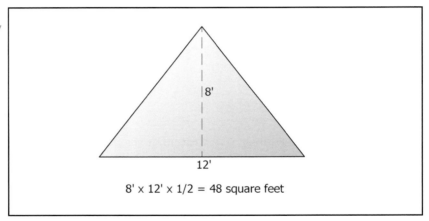

8'

12'

8' x 12' x 1/2 = 48 square feet

Figure 5.5 In a rectangle with an offset, calculate the square footage for the two rectangular areas and add them together.

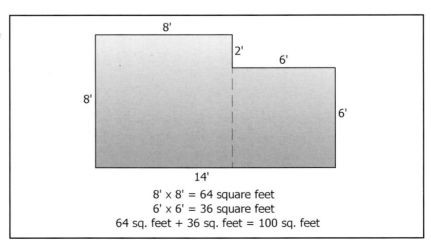

8'

2'

6'

8'

6'

14'

8' x 8' = 64 square feet
6' x 6' = 36 square feet
64 sq. feet + 36 sq. feet = 100 sq. feet

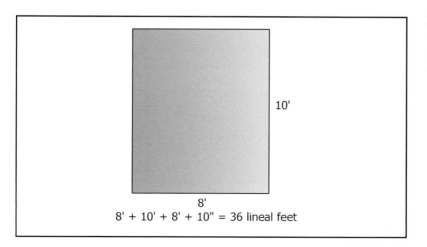

8' + 10' + 8' + 10" = 36 lineal feet

Figure 5.6 To calculate lineal footage, simply add up the footage on all sides and the total is the lineal footage.

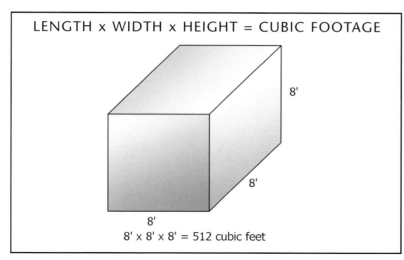

LENGTH x WIDTH x HEIGHT = CUBIC FOOTAGE

8' x 8' x 8' = 512 cubic feet

Figure 5.7 and 5.8 To calculate cubic footage, multiply length x width x height.

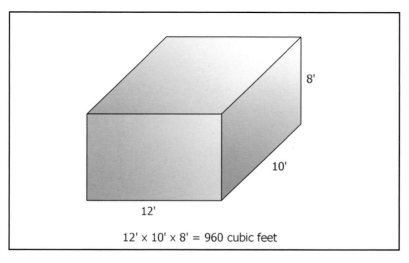

12' x 10' x 8' = 960 cubic feet

TIPS FROM THE MASTERS –
Basic Estimating Checklist Suggestions

1. Make a site inspection, identifying and quantifying every specific step in the project.

2. Use a predetermined unit costing/pricing system to derive the total for each item to be performed.

3. Where a unit price is not available, determine the material cost and labor estimate as accurately as possible.

4. Use a predetermined unit costing/pricing system to derive the total for every subcontract item.

5. Where a unit price is not available on subcontract work, contact the appropriate subcontractor or supplier to provide the necessary information.

6. Where the final decision has not been made on a specification, use an allowance figure based on installer's cost, or delete the item from the estimate.

7. Review the entire project and make a judgment on all unusual job conditions, including, at least:

   • Access to work location.

   • Materials storage requirements.

   • Geographic factors, including travel, parking, jurisdictional licensing requirements.

   • Time requirements for starting or completion.

   • Installer's familiarity with the type of job and materials being used.

   • Client requirements, including negotiation stance, standards of performance, talkativeness, neatness expectations, other idiosyncrasies.

   • Current workload and availability of subcontractors.

   • Availability of materials, special order items.

   • Presence of a third-party supervisor such as an architect.

   Then convert these judgments into a quantitative adjustment to the cost of the job.

8. Calculate job cost to obtain price, based on net profit and overhead requirements.

9. Have another individual review the specifications and estimate, checking for completeness, mathematical accuracy and review of judgment factors. (If no second person is available, wait 24 hours and then review it yourself.)

10. Submit the estimate in proper form to the client and include:

    • Payment schedule

    • Approximate starting and completion dates

    • Time limit on acceptance of the proposal

    • Company acceptance clause

Based on the products specified, jobsite inspections completed and design details agreed to, the project specifications are prepared.

Standard Specifications

One of the best ways to increase productivity in the kitchen and bathroom business is to use standard master specifications. Specifications drawn up from scratch for each project, especially when unfamiliar products are used, require a great deal of time

While it is true that no two jobs are the same, a large percentage of the equipment and work for kitchens and bathrooms is standard. NKBA offers its members a standard specification format for kitchen and bathrooms.

- These standard specifications eliminate vagueness or gray areas that are often found in hastily written specifications.

- Standard specifications also allow for fine-tuning of the estimating system for increased accuracy. As an operation is repeated, using the same method and products, closer attention can be given to labor and materials costs for that particular item and the unit price can be adjusted accordingly.

- Standard specifications are easily adaptable to a computer system. Continually add new specifications so that they can be reused in future projects.

- Standard specifications that call out the use of the same products on a regular basis mean that the design and installation team learn the individual characteristics of each product, and increase their own efficiency during installation of the product. This leads to a reduction in mistakes and an increase in productivity.

- It is much easier to keep abreast of price changes when the standard specifications are written around a limited number of standard products.

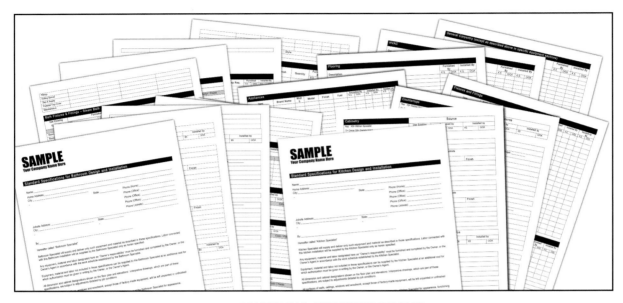

Figure 5.9 *The NKBA Standard
Specifications for Kitchen and Bath
Design and Installation*

MATERIAL SPECIFICATIONS

List the exact equipment and materials for the project by
manufacturer name, model number or specific product description.
Written specifications should acknowledge the problems with
matching between old materials and new materials. Phrases such as
"match as closely as possible within the installer's normal sources of
supply" and "surfaces or materials to blend" are much better than
simply saying "to match."

Example of a Material Specification

- Supply kitchen cabinetry, as per plans and elevations dated
  June 6, 2006, with all specified finished ends, mouldings and
  decorative hardware.

- Cabinets to be X, Y, Z brand, full overlay design with five-piece
  raised panel door style in cherry wood, stained Umbria Brown.

- Cabinet construction to be 3/4 inch sides, tops, bottoms and
  shelves, 1/2 inch back, 45 lb. commercially rated industrial
  board core with white melamine surfaces unless finished sides
  specified in cherry.

- All base and wall shelves to be similar material, finished with
  3 mm PVC edge tape on all four sides. All base and wall
  shelves to be adjustable on 5 mm faces.

- All hinging to be totally concealed, 120 degree opening, low
  profile six-way adjustable, demountable hinging.

- All drawers to be five-piece dovetail drawer boxes with under-mounted, full extension, self-closing drawer slides.

- Decorative hardware to be brushed nickel cup pull on drawers, and brushed nickel 1 1/4-inch pulls on all doors.

PERFORMANCE SPECIFICATIONS

Outline the performance standards required for a particular operation or product.

Example of a Performance Specification

"Supply and install three-piece bathroom within 5 feet of main stack. Bath waste lines and water piping to meet existing codes, including necessary shutoff valves, cleanouts, and back vents." (Exact fixtures and fittings should be specified.)

Performance specifications are best suited for areas in which there are codes to meet or where performance characteristics are clearly understood. In areas where performance characteristics are not specific, this type of specification leaves too much room for disagreement between client and installer.

TECHNICAL SPECIFICATIONS

Technical specifications spell out each operation, detailing requirements for installation of the work.

Example of Technical Specifications

"Build new interior partition to divide existing bathroom into two separate bathrooms. Supply top and bottom plates and studs 16 inch o.c., studs to be Douglas fir construction grade or equal. Install 1/2-inch drywall to manufacturer's specifications, tape all joints and spackle with two coats. Spackle all screw holes. Screws to be standard drywall screws. Install three-piece base, 1 inch x 4 inches #2 pine with ogee and oak shoe mould, shoe mould to be natural. Paint new wall with two coats of top quality paint, vinyl latex on new walls, semi-gloss on all wood trim."

Technical specifications should be used whenever possible, and should include quantities, dimensions and methods. It is perfectly acceptable to use a phrase such as "performed in a worker-like manner."

Specifications for simple work need not be professionally drawn up in order to be descriptive, and they can be a great help in communication between the installer and the client.

HANDLING UNKNOWN HIDDEN CONSTRUCTION CONTINGENCIES

On jobs that are likely to include unknowns that will not be discovered until the job is started, make some provision for their correction. If, for example, in the process of replacing a toilet, the floor covering shows signs that the existing toilet may have been leaking, there is a good possibility that the plywood subfloor may be deteriorated and will require replacement. Rather than have the subflooring replaced on a time-and-material basis, stipulate a cost per square foot for the subfloor replacement, if required. Include provisions for both the additional cost and for preparation of a change order.

CHAPTER 6: A "Win-Win" Strategy

Designers who "win" understand both the design and the installation process. This understanding allows them to produce award-winning projects, on time and on budget. These designers have a strong, ongoing working relationship with trade partners/installers and have satisfied clients, who then refer the designers to others.

WHAT IT TAKES TO WIN

Successful Designers

- Have in-depth product and industry knowledge.

- Participate in the industry, resulting in their ability to spot design trends and new product innovations.

- Create projects based on the accepted guidelines published by the National Kitchen & Bath Association.

Figure 6.1 *NKBA members can access the NKBA Kitchen & Bathroom Planning Guidelines at NKBA.org.*

- Strive to be detail-oriented—or partner with detail-oriented individuals—to develop detailed project documentation, including complete plans and specifications.

- Are great communicators: both during the design and sales process, as well as during the installation process.

- Are organized.

- Realize that their creative conceptual plans are little more than an elegant drawing until they have assembled the team necessary to order, receive and install the individual elements of the kitchen or bath plan.

To create a winning plan, let's walk through a typical kitchen or bath plan in detail.

We have discussed throughout this book the various business models that offer profitable business opportunities in the kitchen and bath industry. Regardless of what type of business model your firm follows, all of the following steps are part of successful projects.

PROJECT PREPARATION

Successful kitchen and bath designers take the following steps to insure profitable projects and satisfied clients.

The Planning and Estimating Process

THE SURVEY

- Identify the client's needs and wants.

- Charge some type of a design retainer.

- Create preliminary design solutions and make preliminary appliance recommendations or—receive and incorporate appliance specifications from the client or the client's agent (builder, architect, interior designer).

THE BUDGET ESTIMATE

Proven, successful professionals talk about the budget early and often. In fact, many seasoned professionals present a "ballpark," "guesstimate" or "price range" to the consumer as early as the first meeting in the showroom. This approach to the business of design is of great value to the consumer because budget is always a concern. Keep in mind that the design and planning process is one-third functional space management, one-third the aesthetic statement, and one-third the funds available.

CONCEPTUAL PRESENTATION

Designers must understand the difference between renovation and new construction, and single-family vs. multi-family housing. During the concept presentation, identify a homeowners' association or any other governing body which needs to be contacted for plan review and approval.

In addition to a homeowners' association or board of directors, major renovation undertakings which include room additions, tear-downs or structural alterations that impact the footprint of the home may need prior approval from the local building department to meet building codes.

During this phase, designers may discuss or present to the consumer disclaimers which detail specific installation and/or building processes they recommend and/or insist on. For example:

- A designer might not provide cabinets for sale unless their firm also provides installation.

- A designer may not continue past the concept design stage until the consumer has completed all of their appliance selections.

- Delicate finishes on bath fittings may not be specified because of water or air quality concerns.

During the concept presentation phase, give the client one or more potential solutions to the space. Show the client a portfolio with photos of completed projects. At these meetings, allow the client to present their ideas for solutions. Encourage them to show pictures they may have gathered.

FINALIZE DESIGN ADJUSTMENTS, APPLIANCE SELECTIONS AND CABINET DECORATIVE SURFACES (INCLUDING HARDWARE)

Wise designers believe a bridge exists between the concept plans and final plans that connects the final selections for the appliances, the cabinet wood specie, finish, artistic enhancements and decorative hardware. These designers know the importance of helping clients make decisions on many of the seemingly small details early in the planning phase.

Oftentimes, clients cannot understand why a designer specifies a dishwasher this early, or whether the choice between a pull and knob makes sense. Seasoned professionals know that these individual elements of a kitchen plan must be selected sooner rather than later to insure that the project progresses smoothly and finishes on time and on budget. Similarly, in bath planning, the inclusion of a steam system in a shower is an important early decision because of its impact on the size of a shower (which now must accommodate a bench or a seat), as well as the wall surround porosity determining the size (and cost) of the generator.

RECEIVE FIRM ESTIMATES

Once the design is detailed enough for the craftspeople who will be responsible for creating the new room to review, schedule and conduct an in-office review of plans or an actual jobsite visit. At that point, firm installation estimates and/or contracts for the installation portion of the project are presented to the design firm, to the builder, or directly to the client.

MATERIAL SELECTIONS/ALLOWANCES

After the client approves the final plan, reviews contract documents and selects cabinets and appliances, a second layer of product selections takes place. (Sometimes the countertop surfaces fall into this second layer.) The client selects the decorative materials in the kitchen or bath at this time, or the designer identifies allowances, which are listed in the contract.

REVIEW DESIGN WITH INSTALLATION SPECIALIST

All projects that involve any construction will typically require a jobsite check and inspection by the installation specialist or the product manager for the design firm. This is particularly critical if the design firm retains contract installation specialists because then an installation contract separate from the material contract is presented to the client.

There can be no "gray" areas—"ballpark" figures are not acceptable at this stage. Good craftspeople will not commit to an installation fee until they have seen the physical jobsite.

CONFIRM ESTIMATES

At this point a double-check of the estimates is an excellent idea.

PREPARE PRESENTATION AND WORKING DRAWINGS

After all of the materials are identified and/or allowances settled on, and all appropriate craftspeople review the project, prepare the actual working drawings, contracts, color boards and other presentation tools.

PRESENT PROJECT AND MAKE FINAL DESIGN ADJUSTMENTS

Present the project to the client. Make final changes to the plan and/or contracts.

SIGN DISCLAIMERS

Clients may need to sign a "specification approval" or a "disclaimer" along with the contract. For example, if clients are ordering natural cherry cabinetry, they may sign a specification approval, acknowledging the inherent color range in natural cherry, which remains even after the finishing process.

SIGN CONTRACT

Review all documentation, stamp the plans "final." The client signs the contract and pays a deposit.

FINAL SURFACES/MATERIALS SELECTIONS MADE OR VERIFIED

Once the cabinets are ordered, the client selects decorative materials such as backsplash tile, light fixtures, and floor materials.

The Scheduling and Ordering Process

As soon as the client signs the contracts, the scheduling and ordering process begins. It is important that the designer or the firm's representative stay in touch with the client between the contract signing and the actual start date. This could be as long as 12 to 24 weeks with some custom cabinet products. Information about such a proactive marketing program can be found in Chapter 10: Marketing of the *Kitchen & Bath Business Management* book from NKBA.

SCHEDULE THE INSTALLATION

Inspect the jobsite, if this was not done earlier.

- Write the cabinet order and transmit after careful comparison to the final jobsite dimension check, and the floor plan to the elevation.

- Schedule the trade contractors' work.

- Complete the permit process.

- Create the jobsite workbook.

PRE-INSTALLATION COMMUNICATION

- The client receives regular updates.

- Begin to include any homeowners' association or other organizations that have control over the jobsite in the scheduling and ordering process.

Notify neighbors or other individuals affected by the work that the project begins soon.

ORDER THE PRODUCT

Many firms have an absolute rule that no project begins until the design firm receives all materials and they are ready to go to the jobsite. Sometimes designers have a hard time understanding this. The inexperienced designer is unaware that, for example, in bathroom remodeling, the shower/tub fittings must be on the jobsite early because the "rough-in valve" is installed during the framing stage. This is far earlier than when the fittings are installed against the finished wall material.

The Installation Process

INSTALLATION BEGINS

- Whomever will be responsible for managing the project inspects the site.

- Deliver materials.

- Complete demolition.

- Remove trash.

- Rough construction and mechanical takes place. (Trash removal is key during each of these steps.)

  1. Footings and Foundations

  2. Framing, Walls and Roof

  3. HVAC

  4. Plumbing/Electrical

  5. Finished Wall Surfaces/Preparation

INSPECTIONS

Building department inspections take place.

FINISH COMPLETED

- The walls are "closed in."

- A second inspection takes place.

- Seal and prime the wall surfaces.

FLOOR INSTALLATION: OPTION 1

In some projects, the finished floor material is installed at this point because it extends throughout the space. Typically, when the floor is installed at this stage, it is then covered with heavy-duty protective materials. In other installations, flooring is installed after all other products. As the designer, it is important that you know which system to use on the project.

CABINETS ARRIVE

Typically, the cabinets are delivered to the jobsite—either boxed or blanket wrapped. Think through the jobsite access required by a large delivery truck. How will the cabinetry be removed from the truck tailgate (and by whom)? What path from the truck tailgate to the storage area or work zone will be followed (particularly important in inclement weather)? These are all important things to consider at the delivery phase.

At this stage, the second major payment is usually due.

INSTALL CABINETS AND ALL DECORATIVE HARDWARE

This is an important time for the designer to meet with the client and review the project. Seasoned professionals suggest the following:

- Set an appointment with the client, preferably when natural light illuminates the room and after artificial lighting is installed so that the light levels that will be in place when the room is finished can be simulated for the inspection. Note: Sometimes, a client will use a construction light to carefully inspect every square inch of the cabinet surface. Other clients review each cabinet as it comes off the truck. Neither of these inspection techniques is proper. Inspect materials under the same light levels expected within the space and at a standing distance of 36 inches. (See Chapter 2.)

- If payment is due at this time, smart designers also alert the client they will be bringing an invoice. Now is a good time to review change orders and to take care of other paperwork.

167

Structure the appointment by suggesting that you first review the project, and then retire to another part of the dwelling (or outside—it might be inside a warm car) to review the documents. If there is a temporary jobsite office, this is an excellent meeting area.

- This is an ideal time to begin the punchlist process. A list of suggestions from seasoned professionals appears in Chapter 2. Start developing the list in one corner of the room and methodically review the entire project—with the client—to identify items that may be of concern. Review those items one-by-one and identify as:

  - Acceptable according to industry standards. (Be prepared to have some documentation.)

  - Repair/replacement/rework to accomplish before presenting the final invoice.

  - Warranty work not affecting the final payment. This is work that falls under the timeframe of the warranty.

  - An expectation issue to resolve later with the client.

Unrealistic expectations of the client during the punchlist process can be a touchy subject. If the client expects something that is not possible to deliver, the designer needs to determine just what is causing the unrealistic expectation. Was the client "oversold?" Or is the stress and frustration of a new construction or remodeling project getting the best of the client? Seasoned professionals suggest getting the entire punchlist first so that you can determine the percentage of realistic issues vs. non-realistic issues. Do not attempt to settle each item as you work around the room. Rather, complete the list and then begin on the items, one by one. Frequently, the unrealistic expectations can then be isolated and dealt with separately. The solution may revolve around a product defect and the product might be replaced at minimal expense to the designer. Aim to satisfy the client quickly and professionally.

PROJECT PUNCHLIST—DRAFT 1

Complete the first punchlist draft. It is important for everyone to realize the building business and the renovation industry is not an exact science. Reassure the clients that you have their best interests at heart. Carefully detail any work to be replaced, reworked and/or redesigned early so these changes can be designed, engineered, costed, ordered and received in tandem with the continuing work at the jobsite.

TEMPLATE COUNTERTOPS

For some design firms, the countertop order is placed along with the cabinets and the countertop may be onsite. But it is more typical that the countertops are templated (or measured) after the cabinets are installed.

FINISH DECORATIVE SURFACES

Because there is down time between the countertop templating and its fabrication and installation, this is usually the ideal time to finish all trim work and decorative surface finishing.

INSTALL COUNTERTOPS

Finally, the client can begin to see what their new space looks like.

INSTALL BACKSPLASH

The backsplash is installed.

FLOOR INSTALLATION: OPTION 2

If flooring option 2 was chosen, the floor is finished now.

PROJECT PUNCHLIST—DRAFT 2

Create Draft 2 of the project punchlist.

INSTALL APPLIANCES, FIXTURES AND FITTINGS

Connect appliances, fixtures and fittings.

PROJECT PUNCHLIST—FINAL

Create the final punchlist with the owner and the owner's agent.

COMPLETE DECORATIVE SURFACES

Install final decorative surfaces. Touch up those materials finished earlier.

INSTALL LIGHTING FIXTURES

Install all lighting fixtures.

COMPLETE PROJECT PUNCHLIST

Review the final punchlist and complete the work. Present the final invoice.

COMPLETE THE INSPECTION PROCESS

Complete the final "Certificate of Occupancy."

At this juncture, the room can probably be inhabited. This is the normal definition of "substantial completion." Many contracts are written so the final payment is due—at "substantial completion"—allowing the design firm to collect their final payment from the client with the understanding, by both parties, that there may be outstanding punchlist items that need to be completed, as well as some warranty work that may be unfinished.

The Post Installation Review

This can be the most important phase of the project to ensure turning a profit. Regardless of how well or how poorly a project goes, everyone's focus must be on getting the work done, fixing any mistakes, keeping the client happy (to protect your referral) and collecting the last payment.

By consistently conducting post-installation reviews you will be able to identify areas of weaknesses and strengths within your own areas of responsibility as well as that of the organization and subcontractors or contract installers you work with.

POST-INSTALLATION COMMUNICATION

Send a post-installation communication to the client. Present clients with their warranty and perhaps a gift. Thank neighbors for "putting up" with the trucks, tradespeople and all the details of a construction site.

REVIEW PROJECT AND PRESENT FINAL INVOICE

If not accomplished earlier, hold a final review of the project and present the final invoice to the client or the client's agent.

COMPLETE PUNCHLIST AND WARRANTY WORK

Lastly, complete all punchlist, as well as warranty work.

CHAPTER 7: Closing Comments

The entire *Professional Resource Library* created by the National Kitchen & Bath Association is an intertwined body of knowledge that designers must master to be successful. The insights and experiences from practicing professionals shared in this volume represent a unique body of knowledge. Pay particular attention to the highlighted Tips from the Masters.

Our goal is that the combined experience of the author and all contributors to this text will save you from making the same mistakes they did.

These experts stress that creative space planning or the specification of aesthetically beautiful material is only the beginning of a successful kitchen or bath design. Your client cannot drive a kitchen around the block, nor can they try a new bathroom on. They really do not know what they bought until it is installed and paid for. They only fully realize the functionality and beauty of their new space when they cook that first meal or take a wonderful soaking bath.

Because you carefully gathered client information, created detailed project documents, cautiously estimated the project and managed the installation process in an organized manner, your clients will be able to enjoy their first meal or relaxing bath around the forecasted finish date with total satisfaction.

Chapter 3

INDEX